Literature

D0189038

...ul

Nicola Grove

David Fulton Publishers

London

371.9280464 GRO

David Fulton Publishers Ltd
Ormond House, 26–27 Boswell Street, London WC1N 3JD

First published in Great Britain by David Fulton Publishers 1998

Note: The right of Nicola Grove to be identified as the author of this work has been asserted by her in accordance with the Copyright, Designs and Patents Act 1988.

Copyright © Nicola Grove 1998

British Library Cataloguing in Publication Data
A catalogue record for this book is available from the British Library

ISBN 1–85346–495–3

All rights reserved. No part of this publication may be reproduced, stored in a retrieval system or transmitted, in any form, or by any means, electronic, mechanical, photocopying, recording or otherwise, without the prior permission of the publishers.

Typeset by FSH Print and Production Ltd, London
Printed in Great Britain by Bell and Bain Ltd, Glasgow

Contents

Acknowledgements

This book is the outcome of work by lots of different people who have given me ideas and inspiration. In particular I would like to thank the following:

John Haynrych, Headteacher of Kingsbury School, and Lynn Ranson, Advisory Teacher for Secondary English. Their enthusiastic support for literature in special schools has developed great expertise among teachers and support staff. Rosie Brown, Jane Grecic, Sue Lund and all the teachers who attended workshops generated a host of imaginative projects, some of which are described here.

My husband Bob, friends and colleagues Keith Park, Tina and Mike Detheridge, Julie Dockrell and Nick Peacey, who have consistently been prepared to drop everything and read drafts of the book whenever I demanded it. I have borrowed *Tongue Meat* from Keith Park's repertoire of stories. Also my friend Mike Coles and my daughter Ghislaine for their help with the artwork.

Jane Miller, Ann Turvey, Tony Burgess, John Hardcastle and Anton Franks from the Institute of Education, London University, who provided time and space to discuss ideas on assessment and teaching.

Students from various places, including Mapledown School, Heathermount School Kingsbury School and the Ermine Road Day Centre, whose responses made me stop and think – and their teachers and key workers who were prepared to join in and take some risks.

The constructive detailed feedback offered by Edwin Webb helped to clarify my ideas on emotion and perception. Peter Llewellyn-Jones provided valuable advice on translating texts into sign.

'Wind' from *The Hawk in the Rain* by Ted Hughes is reproduced by kind permission of Faber and Faber Ltd.

An extract from *Red Boots On* is reprinted by kind permission of Kit Wright. *Red Boots On* was originally printed in *The Bear Goes Over the Mountain*, published by Salamander.

An extract from *What has happened to Lulu?* by Charles Causley is reprinted by kind permission of David Higham Associates.

An extract from *Exercise Book* is reprinted by kind permission of the Paul Dehn Estate, London Management Ltd.

Extracts from Theodore Roethke's poem 'The Waking', from *Theodore Roethke – Collected Poems,* and Samuel Beckett's 'Breath', from *Collected Shorter Plays of Samuel Beckett*, are reproduced by kind permission of Faber and Faber Ltd.

Material from the English National Curriculum is Crown Copyright and is reproduced by kind permission of the Controller of HMSO.

Appendix 4 is reproduced from the following article with kind permission of Marybeth Allen and Cambridge University Press: Allen, M., Kertoy, M., Sherblom J. and Pettit, J. (1994) 'Children's narrative productions: a comparison of personal event and fictional stories'. *Applied Psycholinguistics,* 15, 149–176.

An extract from Carolyn Fyfe's unpublished *Gulliver's Travels* is reproduced by kind permission of the author.

The stories and poems in Chapter 6 are reproduced with kind permission of the students and teachers who wrote them.

Finally, this book is dedicated to my grandfather, Percival Gurrey, Professor of English and Vice Principal of the University of the Gold Coast, whose teaching in the English Department at the Institute of Education inspired many of the people who taught me. The poetry he read to me as a child is everyone's inheritance.

Nicola Grove
London
July 1998

Introduction

This book offers a practical guide to using novels, plays and poetry with students across the full range of ability and with a particular focus on students with moderate, severe and profound learning difficulties.

Because literature is the art of language, one of the key problems facing teachers is how to use age-appropriate texts with students whose ability to understand and use either written or spoken language is severely limited. *Literature for All* presents a structured framework for selecting and adapting texts, and a variety of rich and imaginative strategies designed by practising teachers for use in the classroom. It is aimed at anyone who enjoys a good tale, however it is told, and would like to extend that experience to all students. The belief which underlies this book is that the best literature has a power which goes beyond words - and that literature is too important to be restricted to those who can read! This has implications for the ways in which literature is introduced to all students – and not just those with learning difficulties. It will be argued that the practical task of seeking to accommodate the needs of some learners challenges received notions of literacy, literature, and the relationship between the two.

These concepts are explored in the first two chapters of the book, which discuss the development of the English curriculum, its assumptions about the teaching of literature and the implications for students who have special educational needs. It is concluded that a curriculum which lays emphasis on a skills-based approach to the development of response to literature will inevitably be exclusive, rather than inclusive. In the third chapter, findings are reviewed which suggest an alternative approach, based on contextual inference and the capacity for emotional response and expression: termed *affect* or feeling. These findings provide the basis of a framework for access to literature for all learners, which is presented in the fourth chapter. The following chapters discuss classroom strategies for using literature and for developing creative writing, using examples from ongoing work in special and mainstream schools, and approaches to assessment and evaluation of student responses.

Starting points

The greatest challenge in adapting literature for special needs is undoubtedly presented by students with profound and multiple learning difficulties – and this is not simply a problem of making the texts accessible. It has more to do with the rationale for the whole activity. Staff who work regularly with these students may feel (justifiably) that it takes every minute of every day and all their energy to achieve the most basic functional participation in everyday life. To take time out from these activities to engage with literature may be seen as at best irrelevant and at worst a denial of their needs. It is my passionate conviction that, on the contrary, poetry and stories address the most fundamental needs of any human being, regardless of their level of disability, and that some of the best opportunities for developing the functional communication skills of students arise in these contexts. It is not necessary to compromise the provision of individual programmes dedicated to cognitive and social skills – rather, the goals for individuals can be incorporated into the sessions for literature (see Grove and Park 1996 for a discussion of these issues and a related assessment framework).

Reversing the principle that 'hard cases make bad law', this book will seek to build a coherent approach to the teaching of literature which takes as its starting point the needs of the student with profound and multiple learning disabilities, using a developmental framework and the principle of partial participation (Baumgart 1992). It will be argued that if we re-examine the roots of language comprehension and expression in early infancy, we can discover principles which will guide us in the adaptation of literature in ways that are appropriate to all learners. It will also be argued, on the basis of the personal experience of people who have tried out some of these approaches, that using literature across the range of ability is energising, fun for everyone involved and can lead to new developments for ourselves as well as for our students.

> The nature of a story – of drama and pretence – is to make us step outside ourselves and start to try out things and to take risks that we otherwise may not be inclined to do. This is what we hope will happen for our students, and maybe it will also happen for ourselves as group leaders. In each of the three stories (*The Odyssey*, *The Hobbit* and *Gulliver's Travels*) the main character embarks on an adventure which he did not initially intend, and has to deal with more than he bargained for. Through these experiences his horizons are unexpectedly broadened; Odysseus is trying to return home, but is waylaid by goddesses and sea monsters; the Hobbit, Bilbo Baggins, is not an adventurous sort at all, but he is included in an expedition to reclaim treasure from the dragon who stole it; and Gulliver goes on several journeys, but shipwrecks and other disasters land him in the strangest countries. When we, as group leaders, embark on a voyage into the realms of imagination with our groups, perhaps we will find ourselves being stretched in ways we would not have thought possible: and perhaps we shall discover some personal new horizons. (Fyfe 1996)

CHAPTER 1

Literature and the English curriculum

> The struggle of man against power is the struggle of memory against forgetting.
>
> Milan Kundera *The Book of Laughter and Forgetting*

> You are to be in all things regulated and governed...by fact. We hope to have, before long, a board of fact, composed of commissioners of fact, who will force the people to be a people of fact, and nothing but fact. You must discard the word Fancy altogether. You have nothing to do with it. You are not to have, in any object of use or ornament, what would be a contradiction in fact. You don't walk upon flowers in fact; you cannot be allowed to walk upon flowers in carpets. You don't find that foreign birds and butterflies come and perch upon your crockery. You never meet with quadrupeds going up and down walls; you must not have representations of quadrupeds upon walls. You must use...for all these purposes, combinations and modifications (in primary colours) of mathematical figures which are susceptible of proof and demonstration. This is the new discovery. This is fact. This is sense.
>
> Charles Dickens *Hard Times*

English is a fairly recent academic discipline, becoming a university subject only in the twentieth century. To study English has traditionally meant to study literature, as the following quotation implies: 'Literature lies at the heart of the English order. All students have an entitlement to a wide range of literary texts which are challenging and rewarding to read, and which can offer examples of the finest achievement in writing'. (NCC 1991, p.3)

The role of literature is seen as threefold:

- to develop empathy, imagination and insight which will nourish the personal and social growth of individuals;
- to provide shared experience of cultural heritage;
- to develop and extend literacy skills.

(DES 1989; DES 1988)

Through reading texts which excite interest and empathy, and which provide different models of writing, students' literacy will develop – not just functional reading and writing, but their familiarity with the huge variety of ways in which experience may be expressed in different situations. These aims seem laudable enough – and yet the teaching of English is so intimately bound up with both cultural and national identity that it has always been a politically sensitive subject. The history of the development of the English curriculum in England and Wales has significant implications for the way in which literature is defined, and this in turn affects curricular access for students with special educational needs. In its current form (DES 1995), there is very little reference to the way in which the subject is conceptualised, or of appropriate methods of teaching. Ideas about literature and language and the relationship between them are presented as received opinion in the English orders, but in fact they represent one particular perspective, which has been vigorously criticised (Cox 1995; Knight 1996). It is relevant to discuss the development of the ideas which underpin the design of the English curriculum, in order to identify where the problems may occur when we start to think about creating meeting points between the text and the individual student. Although the historical background that follows relates only to the specific circumstances of England and Wales, there are some general conclusions to be drawn which may have a wider application.

The English National Curriculum

English was one of the first subjects to be developed within the National Curriculum for England and Wales, after the Education Reform Act of 1988. The original curriculum came in the form of a report from the working group chaired by Brian Cox (DES 1989) which was in turn based on the findings of the Kingman Committee into the teaching of English language, in 1988.

The Kingman Report (DES 1988)

The Kingman Committee was set up to recommend a model of English language which would serve as the basis for the English National Curriculum, drawing on the findings of the Bullock Report (1975). The model which was proposed had four levels (see Figure 1.1): forms of spoken and written language (sounds, words, sentence structure and discourse structure); features of the communication process (speakers, listeners and context); principles of acquisition and development, and principles of historical and geographic variation.

The committee examined the role of language, as conceptualised in this model, in relation to social and linguistic needs, conceptual and intellectual development, and aesthetic and literary awareness. Its recommendations were essentially concerned with the use of language for *communication*, defined as understanding and expression for a particular purpose, in the context of a particular audience. The focus was on language which is functional, enabling young people to achieve and contribute in society, as the following quotation makes clear: 'Children who read Tolkien and then write their own fairy stories are engaged in a total process of language development which, among other advantages, may one day contribute to the writing of clear, persuasive reports about commerce or science' (para. 19).

Hence there was a pervasive concern that all children should be taught the accurate use of standard English in speech and writing. The basic premise of the report was that children need to be socialised into appropriate uses of language, and, although there was some acknowledgement of the need to value children's own experience and linguistic background, this was little more than a formality. Indeed, the committee expressly rejected that school of thought which gained prominence in the 1960s, that teachers of English needed to put the child, rather than the canon, at the centre of their work:

It is not enough to write 'freely' with no thought given to the audience for the writing, or the shape and patterns of the language used... (para. 20).

It is possible that a generation of children may grow up deprived of their entitlement – an introduction to the powerful and splendid history of the best that has been thought and said in our language. Too rigid a concern with what is relevant to the lives of young people seems to us to pose the danger of impoverishing not only the young people, but the culture itself, which has to be revitalised by each generation (para. 22).

The Kingman Report set out attainment targets in the areas of speaking, reading and writing, all of which focus on clear and unambiguous communication in standard English. The final recommendations of the Report led to the setting up of a working group, chaired by Brian Cox, to formulate proposals for a National English Curriculum.

---

1. The forms of the English language

speech and writing

(word forms, phrase and sentence structure, discourse structure)

---

2. Communication and comprehension

context, speakers and listeners

---

3. Acquisition and development

aspects of language are acquired gradually, and across different timespans

---

4. Historical and geographical variation

language changes over time

there are regional variations in language

Figure 1.1 *The Kingman Committee model of language*

The Cox Report (DES 1989)

The working group took the Kingman model, and developed sets of attainment targets and associated programmes of study for students aged 5–16. Three fundamental and interactive 'profile components' were identified:

- listening and speaking
- reading
- writing

Handwriting and spelling were originally included as separate attainment targets, although in later versions, these were subsumed under writing. Literature was located in the profile component of reading.

The language skills which underpinned these components were defined as *transactional* – that is, with getting things done; and *social* – that is, with maintaining interpersonal relations. They were listed as:

- to put forward and interpret statements of personal feeling, opinions and views;
- to give accurately, to assimilate, and to act appropriately on, information, explanations and instructions;
- to communicate imaginatively and effectively as performers and readers;
- to function collaboratively in discussion;
- to develop awareness of language.

The Cox Report, no less than the Kingman Report, was concerned with effective communication and literacy. However, Cox interpreted these terms more flexibly than Kingman, specifying an imaginative diversity of contexts and teaching approaches, and including separate sections on Literature, Drama and Media studies. Cox also recommended that the literary texts offered in schools should be selected from a wide range of cultures: writings in English, rather than English writers.

In 1993, the National Curriculum Council reviewed the English orders, drawing on feedback from teachers and associated groups. In this version, no fundamental changes were made to the model, but there were changes to the profile components, with the introduction of 'strands' representing sub-skills of speaking and listening, reading and writing. One of these sub-skills was 'response to literature', which, although located within the statements of attainment for Reading, considered response separately from the other skills of *initial reading* (decoding of text), *comprehension* and *information handling*. Far more detailed guidance was provided on the development of particular skills and their assessment, and a controversial list of recommended authors was provided, including contemporary writers of children's fiction, women authors, and authors from different cultural traditions. It was noted by several commentators that the tone of the Revised Orders was more prescriptive than that of Cox, laying an emphasis on the acquisition and practice of skills, rather than engagement in a process of learning. (Cox 1995; Hester, 1993).

In the Dearing Report (1994), with its brief to simplify and cut down on the work load for teachers, most of these innovations were rejected. A range of different types of literature, rather than specific books or authors, was prescribed at KS1 and KS2, but at KS3 and KS4 there was the same list of recommended authors as was proposed in the original curriculum at KS4 – mostly pre-20th century playwrights and novelists.

The role of literature in Kingman and Cox

The National Curriculum was conceived explicitly to establish some uniformity, raise standards, and (certainly in English) re-institute values that were seen as traditional, after what was perceived as an anarchic phase of English teaching in the 1960s which had encouraged the reading of contemporary texts felt to be more accessible to children from a wide range of social backgrounds, and a focus on the development of creativity at the expense of accuracy. These traditional values included an accepted canon of 'good' literature, and a focus on standard English. Kingman was primarily concerned with re-establishing a literary canon, and with the promotion of critical analysis of how writers use language. Cox had a wider perspective:

> An active involvement with literature enables students to share the experience of others. They will encounter and come to understand a wide range of feelings and relationships, by entering vicariously the worlds of

others, and in consequence they are likely to understand themselves (DES 1989, para. 7.3).

However, it is absolutely apparent that for Cox, as for Kingman, the main function of encounters with literature was to improve children's uptake of language that is politically and culturally sanctioned:

> Wide reading, and as great an experience as possible of the best imaginative literature, are essential to the full development of an ear for language . . . (DES 1988, para. 2.21)

> Literature has a number of important roles to play in improving abilities in writing and speaking and listening as well as in developing the child's imagination and aesthetic sense (DES 1989, para.7.8)

Note that 'as well as'. The point is that no committee was ever established to explore how the child's imagination and aesthetic sense are developed through literature – the process is taken as read, as unproblematic, as an aside in the framing of a rationale for teaching and learning. The result is a curriculum essentially utilitarian in its attitude to stories, drama and poetry (Knight 1996). The overriding concern for both Kingman and Cox, was with the *transactional* – with what is functional and achieves an end, in the public sphere. You will search in vain for any reference to ways of educating students in the language of feeling – in how to express themselves with passion and sensitivity, or how to become confident enough, and motivated enough, to write creatively for themselves. Such terms hardly appear in our English curriculum. There is no exploration whatsoever of what it might mean to communicate imaginatively, although this is a stated goal. This has a particular impact on access for students with special needs, who are unlikely ever to master the language skills deemed essential to the study of literature, and who are likely to end up in the same state as Sissy Jupe, in the opening chapter of *Hard Times*.

'Cecilia Jupe. Let me see. What is your father?'

'He belongs to the horse-riding, if you please sir.'

Mr. Gradgrind frowned, and waved off the objectionable calling with his hand.

'We don't want to know anything about that here. Your father breaks horses, don't he? . . . Give me your definition of a horse.'

(Sissy Jupe thrown into the greatest alarm by this demand.)

'Girl number twenty unable to define a horse!' said Mr. Gradgrind, for the benefit of all the little pitchers. 'Girl number twenty possessed of no facts, in reference to one of the commonest of animals! Some boy's definition of a horse. Bitzer, yours.' . . .

'Quadruped. Gramnivorous. Forty teeth, namely, twenty four grinders, four eye-teeth and twelve incisive. Sheds coat in the spring; in marshy countries, sheds hoofs too. Hoofs hard, but requiring to be shod with iron. Age known by marks in mouth.'

Thus (and much more) Bitzer.

'Now, girl number twenty,' said Mr. Gradgrind. 'You know what a horse is.'

Charles Dickens

Critical voices were raised in 1988 and after, in response to Kingman, Cox and the Revised Orders of 1993. For example, Harold Rosen (1988), in an impassioned attack, pointed out the political context of the debate, the lack of attention paid to current linguistic and literary theories and the way in which literature had been sidelined and its role suborned:

> It has come to this then, that we must sell Tolkien and the writing of stories on the grounds that marketable prose may be developed from them. But the direct role of verbal art (imagination working through language) must not be reduced to one of many advantages, but seen as justifiable in its own right (1988, p.18).

And here are the views of teachers, writers and storytellers, responding to the 1993 revisions.

> The new English national curriculum...would be one that ignored most of what has been discovered about the development and teaching of oral and written language over the past thirty years. It would be based on an unreal vision of what the children were like and how best they can be taught. It would be imposed on the experts on the ground, against a strong consensus of professional advice. (Barrs *et al.* 1993)

This overview of the arguments which have surrounded the development of the English National Curriculum reminds us that it represents only one way of looking at the subject, and is a highly selective approach to the study of literature – from the perspective of its usefulness in promoting the skilled use of language. Although the curriculum is due to be revised over the next two years, it seems safe to say that this basic premise is unlikely to change, particularly given the high profile focus on devoting an hour a day to literacy teaching, in order to raise achievement in reading and writing.

Alternative, richer frameworks for the teaching of English are provided by other curricula. For example, the curriculum for English in Scotland provides an exemplary rationale for the teaching of literature and specifically identifies separate strands for 'talking about feelings', 'reading for enjoyment', 'personal writing' and 'imaginative writing'.

The key assumptions about literature in the English National Curriculum can be summarised as follows:

- response to literature is a sub-skill of reading;
- literature should be used to develop literacy skills;
- the discourse to be mastered is that of critical evaluation.

Some of these assumptions will need to be challenged in order to develop real access for students with difficulties in language and learning.

Literature and students with special educational needs

The advent of the National Curriculum opened up the teaching of a range of subjects for students with special educational needs (see, for example, Carpenter, Ashdown and Bovair 1996). However, if we are to avoid tokenistic approaches to inclusion, we have to be prepared to address some of the subject-specific problems which accompany subject-specific opportunities. Within the English curriculum, there are particular challenges in providing access to age-appropriate literature for students whose special needs are associated with difficulties in language and learning. These include: students with moderate, severe and profound learning difficulties; students with specific language and communication difficulties; students with hearing impairments; students whose difficulties fall within the autistic spectrum and students with specific difficulties in reading and writing.

All of these students will find it hard to read and write about literary texts, but the underlying problem for all groups except the last is more fundamental than this: for literature is the art of language, and delays or impairments to the understanding and use of spoken language will have a profound impact on the ability of such students to appreciate and respond to novels, plays and poetry. This is likely to be the case even if written texts are by-passed, and access is provided through story-telling and drama. Although there is an obvious appeal in the statement by the National Curriculum Council (1992) that: 'Students of different ages can respond to the same text in ways that are appropriate to their particular stage of development. What matters is how the invitation to respond is framed...', there is currently a real lack of explicit advice about how such 'framing' can best be done. It is still all too common to find that the only literature available to young people with severe learning difficulties is in the form of picture books designed for nursery children, and to observe a class of sixteen year olds listening to Eric Carle's *The Very Hungry Caterpillar*. I hasten to state at this point that we can all enjoy *The Very Hungry Caterpillar* from time to time. The problem is not that students are presented with a text whose content is not age-appropriate – but it will be a problem if this is the only kind of text their teachers feel able to use.

This book focuses on creative ways of providing access to literature for all learners, regardless of their level of ability. Such a commitment forces us to confront some difficult issues which must be debated and resolved if the enjoyment of literature is to be a genuinely inclusive option within the curriculum and not purely tokenistic. Some of the questions raised are:

- how is 'literature' to be defined?
- what is involved in the comprehension of a text?
- what counts as a response to literature?

The next chapter of this book seeks to address these issues by developing a philosophy and a framework in which to ground practical approaches to adapting texts. In terms of texts, literature is defined as stories or novels, plays and poetry from all places and all times. The only criterion is that the text you choose should be one that you have enjoyed reading, hearing or seeing, and one that you passionately want to share with your students. You will find, however, that the focus of this book is on the choice of texts for students of secondary age and adults, since this seems to be where the major gap exists in age-appropriate resources.

CHAPTER 2

Literature in our lives

> Once upon a time, two rich merchants who were friends married two beautiful girls who were sisters. Every week the merchants visited each other to talk and smoke the hookah. One merchant noticed that whilst his wife seemed to be getting thinner by the day, his friend's wife grew plump, sleek and shining. He asked his friend the secret of his marital success.
>
> 'Why,' his friend replied, 'I give her the meat of the tongue.'
>
> The first merchant hurried home to his wife. Lovingly he prepared a new dish each day starting with lamb tongues and calf tongues. When his wife failed to put on weight, he tried more exotic dishes – lark tongues, chinchilla tongues and peacock tongues. Still his wife grew thinner and thinner. So the merchant proposed to his friend that they should exchange wives for a while. Over the weeks he watched as his own wife – now living with his friend – grew plump and satisfied, whilst his friend's wife, despite all his best efforts, drooped and pined. In desperation he asked his friend to meet him at the baths, and there in the steam room, with plenty of time to explore the subject, he asked him for exact details of the magic recipe of the meat of the tongue.
>
> 'Settle down,' said his friend, 'and listen. Once upon a time...'
>
> (Adapted from *Tongue Meat*, traditional Swahili story retold by
> **Angela Carter**, *The Virago Book of Fairy Tales*.)

Why literature?

Literature may seem an irrelevance to many teachers working with students who have learning difficulties. The emphasis in the English curriculum for special educational needs has always been placed on the development of functional skills in communication and literacy – and it may be argued that 'doing Shakespeare' is a waste of time when a person cannot even make a basic request through gesture or eye pointing. Although stories are used extensively with younger children in special schools, teachers seem to read or tell stories less frequently to older students. This may partly be because of the lack of age-appropriate resources, but perhaps storytelling and literature are also not seen as critical to the social and educational development of students with special needs. Stories tend to function something like sweets – an occasional treat rather than the basis of the diet.

However, there is an alternative argument: that narrative and poetry are fundamental to our emotional and cognitive functioning, providing the means by which we make sense of our experiences and relate to those of others (Grove and Park 1997). An illustration of this is provided in the fable quoted above. Its moral is stark: without stories we will die – perhaps not literally, but imaginatively and emotionally. The following anecdotes may demonstrate the potential relevance of literature in the lives of young people with learning disabilities.

Suleiman and Rahila

These two young people were in their last year at school, and had fallen in love. Suleiman was a good-looking, streetwise young Muslim with quite severe difficulties in the understanding of language, masked by a superficial mastery of social conventions. Rahila was a Hindu girl with moderate learning difficulties, from a very over-protective and orthodox family. Suleiman had a place in a sheltered employment scheme, but Rahila was returning home for good. There was no chance at all of their even meeting or corresponding, let alone taking the relationship any further. As it happened, two teachers in the school were drama enthusiasts, and put on a production of *Romeo and Juliet*, *West Side Story* style, with Suleiman and Rahila playing the leads. The events of the play dramatised their own situation with great poignancy.

David

David was attending a weekly group focusing on self-advocacy skills. He had strong views about some of the things that were going on in his day centre, including experiences of severe bullying. Unfortunately, his speech was extremely unintelligible, and was combined with a limited awareness of other people's reactions. He tended to hold forth in a monologue, and it was hard to respond to his concerns. On one occasion he was speaking at some length about an incident when I suddenly caught the word 'dagger'. My immediate reaction was horror – had the assaults changed from verbal to physical? I asked him to repeat what he had said. His actual words were, 'It was like a dagger in my heart'. David was using poetic language to express his feelings – but I had thought he must be describing a real attack, because I had not expected that a person with learning disabilities could use a figure of speech.

Language provides us with a means of communication, but we define this too often in terms of functional goals, such as requesting and attention-seeking. In fact, both of these purposes can be achieved with reasonable success without recourse to a system of language at all. Suppose the origins of language are nothing to do with requesting – but the sharing of experience, both emotional (Bloom 1993) and social narrative or gossip (Dunbar 1997)? This changes our view of goals in language and communication development, and suggests that our starting points might lie with storytelling and conveying feelings, rather than with requesting and labelling. Literature is fundamentally concerned with the sharing of experience, and this is why it has been traditionally viewed as central to the English curriculum. Fitzpatrick (1988, p. 108) writes of the value that may be conferred through even limited access to an imagined world:

> The delighted recognition of ourselves in others and others in ourselves is one of the most potent insights literature can afford; and though younger children are not likely to register such moments in quite the same conscious way that older children or adults might, the possibility is nevertheless there for an increased awareness of the shared lineaments of our disparate natures.

If students with special educational needs are to have access to a broad and balanced curriculum, it follows that provision of access to literature should be a primary concern for teachers. Our approach to teaching literature to students who may be able neither to read nor write, nor understand much of what is read to them, will be determined by the way we conceptualise the subject: as an aspect of literacy, an aspect of language or a form of art.

The nature of
literature

In the previous chapter it was argued that the way in which the English curriculum was developed led to an emphasis on the use of language and literacy for functional communication at the expense of the aesthetic. Thus, in a utilitarian definition which Mr. M'choakumchild, in *Hard Times*, (see p. 1) would have relished, the aims for the programmes of study state that the purpose of reading literature is to extend students' skills in literacy:

To develop as effective readers, students should be taught to:

- read accurately, fluently and with understanding;
- understand and respond to the texts they read;
- read, analyse and evaluate a wide range of texts, including literature from the English literary heritage and from other cultures and traditions.

(DES 1995)

Response to literature is located within the programmes of study for reading and writing, suggesting that access to *literature* is inseparable from access to *literacy*. This principle is exemplified in the National Literacy Strategy (DfEE 1998). The focus here is on the development of reading and writing skills, involving strategies at three levels: words, sentences and texts. Again, it is clear that stories and poetry are conceptualised as the vehicles through which literacy is to be developed. This is particularly clear in the scheme of work for reception classes (the rising fives), where most of the aims relate to the ability to recognise connections between print and meaning, or conventions of story composition. Given the investment of time and money in the project, and the pressure on the curriculum, there is a real danger that the study of literature will effectively be ghettoised to the literacy hour. This leaves no space to experience story or poetry *for its own sake*. Shared reading of 'Big Books' and poetry posters is no substitute for story reading by a good teacher, or dramatisations developed by pupils.

Although the connection between literature and literacy is obvious, it is an open question whether it is also a *necessary* connection. Writing is, of course, a convenient way of giving literature a permanence of form and communicating with a wider audience, yet access to literature is not entirely dependent upon the ability to read or write. Dixon (1994) points out (p. 6) 'the tradition of silent reading, I believe, has tended to marginalise our knowledge that for most of its life, literature has been treated as performance', and goes on to argue that print is not equivalent to speech, but only a representation of it. Print omits the vocal dimensions which give meaning to an utterance through rhythm, intonation, pitch, stress and timbre.

It is only in this century (and in the Western hemisphere), that literacy has become widespread enough for us to assume that in order to experience or to create 'literature', a person must be able to read and write. The groundlings at the Globe theatre, the crowds who listened to the *Iliad* or *Beowulf*, or who gathered to watch *Oedipus Rex* or the York Mystery plays, the audiences for the Mahabaratha in contemporary village India, or for *Sizwe Bansi is dead* in Johannesburg in the 1970s may not have been literate in the functional sense of the term; but they were and are capable of becoming engaged in works of literature. The earliest literature existed in oral form long before it was written down. Poetry as well as drama was originally a performance art, lyrics being the expression of personal emotion in song, epics and narratives being declaimed or sung like the border ballads of the sixteenth century.

Literature can be transmitted through a multitude of forms, which immediately opens up access for students who cannot read or write. It seems likely that far more people will ultimately access the classics through film, televised and audio-recordings, than will ever read the originals. In fact this principle was recognised in the Cox Report, which recommended that access to Shakespeare's plays be provided in a variety of media, referring to:

> ... exciting, enjoyable approaches that are social, imaginative and physical. This can also be achieved by: use of film and video recordings, visits to live theatre performances, participation in songs and dances, dramatic improvisations, activities in which Shakespeare's language is used by students interacting with each other. (DES 1989, para. 8.9)

In its interpretation of literacy, the Cox Report had its sights on the next millennium and the 'new literacies' of electronic as well as print media: an emphasis firmly rejected by the authors of the more conservative 1995 English curriculum. We therefore need to define the term 'literacy' widely to include more than traditional print. Many students with special needs will also need alternative forms of communication and writing, such as manual signs or graphic symbols.

If literature is not to be equated with book reading, what is the proper context for its study? For some years it has been argued that the study of literature belongs properly with other arts subjects, such as music, drama, dance, film and graphic art, since literature is an aesthetic and not a functional subject (Abbs 1987; Webb 1992). Stories, plays and poetry need to be rescued from the context of functional language study, and restored to the personal territory of imagination and desire (Franks 1996).

The term *aesthetics* comes from the Greek, meaning 'things perceptible through the senses', and it is the discipline concerned with the education of emotion, perception and imagination, in the contemplation and the making of works of art. The aesthetic response is grounded in sensory and affective experiences, and informed and refined through the cognitive operations of reflection and evaluation – what Wordsworth famously called 'emotion recollected in tranquillity'. The arts are concerned with forms of symbolic expression which unite the creative evocation of feeling with technical skill, in the context of cultural traditions. These three elements are seen as essential to aesthetic education, if art is to avoid self-indulgence, sentimentality and superficiality:

Literature as an art form

> Art is embodied symbolic expression and demands knowledge and skill, a formal context and a continuous culture. It includes and transcends the creative play of the growing child... In stimulating feelings without sufficient reference to technique and traditional achievements, we tend to cheapen and exhaust the psyches of our culture. (Abbs 1987 p. 43–45)

Considering literature as an art form suggests that it can be experienced at a physical level, just like a painting, a piece of music, a film or dance. In the context of a curriculum which consistently emphasises the exercise of cognition over feeling and imagination, to speak of the physicality of text strikes a radical note. Yet, as the following quotations make plain, the appeal of a poem or a story lies in its ability to excite the audience in a way which is first and foremost sensory:

However high art may aspire, it is yet always rooted in a bodily response and primitive engagement. (Abbs 1987: 54)

Aesthetic competence is built basically upon perceptions through the senses...These perceptions will be simple or complex, confused or clear according to such things as the sensitivity of the perceptual apparatus... (Goodman 1981)

A poem begins as a lump in the throat, a homesickness, a love sickness. It finds the thought and the thought finds the word. (Robert Frost)

...the poet undertakes to 'know' the world not by exegesis or demonstration or proofs, but directly as a man knows apple in the mouth (Archibald Macleish 1961)

Oh for a language of sensation rather than thought! (John Keats)

Webb (1992), building on the work of D.W. Harding, describes the evolution of the aesthetic response as a gradual transition from sensation to feeling, to cognition. An encounter with the words evokes sensations, physiological responses, which generate affective states – of excitement, fear, contentment, loss. Through active contemplation of the interaction between the art form and our reactions to it, we bring our cognitive faculties into play, so that our response is both emotional and intellectual. Our ability to evaluate a work of art is dependent on our ability to engage with it at a physical and emotional level.

We can therefore look at literature as an aesthetic activity, located within the arts curriculum. Ross (1978) defines the purpose of arts education as emotional development through the creation of expressive forms. This involves introducing students to works of art which will extend their imaginative experience, and teaching them to 'master the raw materials of self-expression in the arts'. The process begins with education of sensuous responses: 'help them to look and see, listen and hear, touch and feel, move and sense their own moving, encounter each other dramatically and be aware of each other's enacting'. What develops in this context, Ross argues, is a special kind of meaning – aesthetic, sensuous meaning, the relationship of one sensation to another, which does not necessarily have to be conceptually mediated. Ross calls it 'intelligent sensing', the transformation of feeling into form. It is this integrity of feeling and form which lies at the heart of the appeal of artistic products: the smooth loving curves of Rodin's entwined couple, the choice of rhythm and images in Macbeth's soliloquy, quoted on p. 26; the quality of light in Vermeer's painting of a girl poised and turning back for a second, as it might be when her name is called in a crowd. Ross suggests that the process of sensitising students to the relationship between feelings and forms takes place within an interaction – originally that safe space between infant and mother where play evolves. It is a process of dialogue, which we will find useful when it comes to deciding how to evaluate the responses of our students to the experiences which we provide. Meanings are explored and created within this interactive space, through the careful structuring and framing of experience provided by the nurturing adult.

Ross's model provides us with a very appropriate basis for working with people who are heavily dependent on sense impressions. However, it may be argued that his individualised approach ignores the wider social context in which art forms are shared. Geertz (1983) suggests that art forms are always the product of cultural systems, and that:

to study an art form is to explore a sensibility, that such a sensibility is essentially a collective mechanism, and that the foundations of such a formation are as wide as social existence, and as deep... [Art forms] materialise a way of experiencing, bring a particular cast of mind out into the world of objects, where men can look at it. (p. 99)

At its simplest, this means that art always has a social context. If we put together Geertz's theory that art forms are the product of 'local knowledge' with the argument that reading literature always involves a process of active creation of meaning in the encounter between the reader and the text, we can, I think, begin to build a model of aesthetic response to literature which encompasses not only the private, individual development of feeling, and the objective quality of the forms through which feelings are expressed, but also the impact of a response on the creation of meaning for the group. We will explore the nature of the expressive response in more depth when we come to consider evaluation and assessment, in the final chapter of this book.

In developing access to literature as an aesthetic experience, therefore, we are providing opportunities for individuals to experience and create meanings that are culturally significant within their particular contexts, as well as in the wider communities to which they belong. Relationships between form and feeling have to be contextualised in order to be perceived.

The reinstatement of feeling and sensation as the basis of response to literature changes how we think about the understanding of texts, in ways which are extremely helpful when we come to consider the difficulties faced in decoding complex language by students with special educational needs. It means that we need to make a distinction between *apprehension* and *comprehension*, as the following quotation from Webb (1992) makes clear:

In art the images of the art-form enable us to make an immediate sensuous apprehension. This is not to say that we will immediately understand a given work, that we shall be able to render it into paraphraseable meaning. But it does mean, as Eliot said of the poem, that we shall be able to apprehend it before we come to comprehend it. (pp. 25–26)

In fact, many of the most powerful texts defy our attempts at paraphrase. At the beginning of *The Winter's Tale*, there is a speech by Leontes where the syntax is so compacted and dense that even the most academic commentators have difficulty in determining its precise meaning:

Affection! thy intention stabs the centre
With what's unreal thou coactive art,
And fellowst nothing; then 'tis very credent
Thou may'st conjoin with something; and thou dost
And that beyond commission, and I find it,
And that to the infection of my brains
And hard'ning of my brows (Act I: Scene 2)

The meaning here cannot be retrieved by decoding – only by sensing the onslaught of the character's tormented logic: in other words, through a process of sensory apprehension. This insight is remarkably compatible with recent views on the nature of linguistic comprehension and expression. In the following chapter we will explore how models of language acquisition can contribute to the development of a framework for the use of literature across the range of special needs.

CHAPTER 3

Language development: comprehension and expression

> I see it feelingly.
> **William Shakespeare** *King Lear* Act IV, Scene 6, l.149

> We think by feeling. What is there to know?
> I hear my being dance from ear to ear.
> I wake to sleep, and take my waking slow.
> **Theodore Roethke** *The Waking*

Ideas about language development

A conventional way of looking at language development is to view the brain as a processor of information. Language input is perceived through sensory receptors (hearing, vision, touch), and decoded as a sequence of words in context. It is at this point that meanings are assigned. Expressively, an idea arises and is given form in a sequence of words which translate into sounds at the point of production. It is traditional to think of development as an increasing ability to process longer sequences of units. Children start by understanding and producing one word, then two words together, then three, and so on until gradually they are able to understand and produce complex sentences. This hierarchical model is the basis of many influential assessment and intervention programmes, for example the *Derbyshire Language Scheme* (Knowles and Masidlover 1982), or *Living Language* (Locke 1985).

However, it seems to be the case that children use more than one strategy to understand their world and express themselves. In the early 1970s, an influential study by Nelson (1973) revealed that some children expressed themselves early on in whole phrases as well as single words, a style which she termed *expressive*. Since then, studies of both comprehension and expression suggest that the notion of 'apprehension before comprehension' may be as true for language as it is for art.

Comprehension: inference and decoding

The earliest period of language development has been described as affective and social, with infants attending to vocal tone and stress. It is well accepted that infants' understanding is based at first on associations with familiar routines and events: 'Children begin by associating an idea with an episode; words become associated with more or less generalised concepts of objects and events; and at the end of the period, words become associated with one another.' (Bloom 1993)

We do not lose our reliance on our experiential knowledge to make sense of the language we hear and read. There are always two parallel routes to comprehension: linguistic decoding and inference (Sperber and Wilson 1986). We do decode sequences of words, but this is never adequate to retrieve meaning, because there is always a gap between what the speaker intends and what the listener understands, which is filled by inference. In other words, the literal meanings of words have to be enriched by our interpretations of the context: that is both the setting and the personal history and knowledge which we bring to the relationship. There is now a considerable body of research suggesting that knowledge and experience of the world, social context and linguistic information interact dynamically in comprehension (Bishop 1997). Young children seem to pay more attention to contextual cues than syntactic information (Clark 1973). They also rely on stress and intonation, cues to which infants are sensitive very early in their development (Golinkoff and Hirsh-Pasek 1995). When listening to stories, familiarity with structural frameworks helps to build comprehension: 'We understand stories not by adding up the parts, but by bringing to our perception of stories a mental model of how stories work.' (Fox 1993, p. 33).

This 'top-down' approach to the study of language understanding contrasts with the 'bottom-up' decoding model on which the English curriculum is based:

> Appreciation of meaning beyond the literal and an understanding of story structure have gone from Level 3. '*Comprehension*' in this new document appears to refer to no more than the ability to talk about the events in a text, or to raise and lower the voice and change pace appropriately when reading aloud. It has been reduced from the active construction of varied levels of meaning to an act of obedience, concerned only with the extraction of literal meaning to order. (Dombey 1993)

Expression

The combination of global perceptions and sensations and linguistic knowledge which seems to characterise comprehension is also applicable to expressive language development. Although it is true that language is inherently generative and inventive, much of what we communicate is relatively predictable in certain contexts. Nelson (1986) proposed that we associate events with particular *schemata*, or frames of reference, which include *scripts* – the behaviour patterns, both verbal and nonverbal, which we are likely to use in any given situation. Routine phrases such as 'happy birthday' 'how are you?' 'up and down' seem to be acquired as whole units, rather than individually constructed. Young children's knowledge of scripts and routines helps them to associate language and events, and to use language appropriately. Scripts and routines gain their meaning from the strength of the association between an event, and the child's reactions to it – pleasurable, painful, humorous, or sad. Children also seem to enjoy language as a form of play from a very early age, manipulating sounds, rhythms and tones of voice. David Crystal (1997) sees a continuum between the enjoyment by a child with severe learning difficulties of the dramatic contrasts of tones in a game of peep-bo and the 'cerebral bliss' experienced by a reader of James Joyce's *Finnegan's Wake*.

Meaning is therefore grounded in emotion, or affect, which provides the earliest and most fundamental impulse for communication (Bloom 1993). It follows that we can take two routes when adapting literature for students with language difficulties. We can build rich affective associations, using stretches of text as scripts, emphasising the feel of the meaning. This can be regarded as a 'top-down' approach. The second approach is 'bottom-up', and involves decoding meaning through simplification and explanation. The starting point for the top-down approach is to generate an emotional response to the text, and in the next section, we will look more closely at what this involves.

Emotions and the arts

Our understanding of emotional development, and of the connections between art and emotion, has been furthered by research into the neurophysiology of emotion. Goleman (1996) explores the nature of 'emotional intelligence'. Emotional responses are located in the amygdala, limbic structures situated above the brainstem. Individuals who have lost their amygdala through surgery or trauma, lack affect, and there is evidence that the amygdala acts independently of the cortex, or 'thinking' brain. Emotional impressions and memories may thus be evoked even in people whose cognition is impaired or severely delayed – and again, this research suggests that feeling is the precursor to thought rather than the other way around: 'The fact that the thinking brain grew from the emotional reveals much about the relationship of thought to feeling: there was an emotional brain long before there was a thinking one.' (Goleman 1996: 10)

Bloom (1993) reviews literature on the development of emotional expression. The infant is born with the means to express both positive and negative affect. From the earliest signals of 'distress and delight', interest, fear, anger and surprise emerge by about three months. By about the age of five months, babies seem to be able to distinguish happy, sad and angry vocalisations, particularly if given the additional cue of facial expression. There seems to be a core of primary emotions which are recognisable across cultures (see Figure 3.1).

```
Anger
Sadness
Fear
Enjoyment
Love
Surprise
Disgust
Shame
```

Figure 3.1 *Primary emotions (Goleman 1996)*

Bloom suggests that the purpose of language is above all expressive – to give form to states of mind and feeling. Language and feeling go together, with feelings conveyed through nonverbal behaviour, until the child has developed the vocabulary and meta-cognitive ability to talk explicitly about feelings. This close tie up between language and feeling is the basis of literature, and of poetic language such as metaphor. Stripped of affect, stories lose their power. Carol Fox (1993) discusses how the study of children's narratives was transformed by Labov's insight that it was only through feeling and personal involvement that a story became a story rather than a list of events:

> Labov… turned the tables by placing major emotions – fear, danger, excitement, pleasure – at the very heart of what makes a story worth listening to. (p. 27)

A model of story which confines it to the events narrated is a referential model, a Gradgrindian model, rejecting those very elements to do with expression and affects which may have a profound effect on the listener and condition what is recalled. (p. 70)

Bruner (1986) also talks of a complementary relationship between two modes of thought or response: the logical, scientific mode, and the narrative mode of action and feeling, which endows experience with meaning.

Webb offers a continuum of response to art which is relevant to students with learning difficulties. He suggests that response begins with a *sensory experience* (seeing, hearing, touching, tasting or smelling) which gives rise to *feeling*. The distinction between sensation and feeling is that 'Sensation informs us what is there, while feeling assesses what is there' (Arnold 1960, p. 31) – assesses, that is, emotionally, in terms of whether the experience moves, or touches us. At this level, feeling is pre-verbal – experience which is as yet unformulated. Feelings are transformed into *perceptions*, which Webb defines as: 'what we make of what we feel. What we feel, when the feeling is attended to, yields perceptions, by which we know, in an appraisal of the information which we receive.' (p. 78)

A perception, in other words, occurs when selective attention is paired with sensation. It is equivalent to a thought, or insight, which may not as yet be fully formulated.

The next stage comes when there is conscious evaluation or judgement of the feeling and the experience: we step back from the work, rather than being absorbed in it, and appraise both the thing itself and our own reactions to it. This is the stage which Webb refers to as *cognition* – an active, intellectual response.

Webb's continuum is summarised in Figure 3.2, and will be taken up again in the chapter on assessment. In relation to work with students with learning difficulty, the continuum allows us a starting point (in sensation) which is accessible to all students. We can aim to develop our students' responses as far along the process as possible, without excluding anyone who has the capacity for some sensation and affect.

Sensation -> Feeling ->Perception -> Evaluation

Figure 3. 2 *Response continuum*

There is thus a growing consensus about the role of affect, or feelings, in the development of communication and the ability to conceptualise the mental states of other people. This coincides with the move to re-establish feeling and sensation as the ground of response to literature as an art form. By placing emotional response at the centre of our work, we may be able to find ways of reaching students whose intellectual difficulties preclude the development of advanced skills in literacy and decoding.

The implications of this perspective on language development and literature is that we can take two routes to the adaptation of texts. We do not have to depend on the primacy of a cognitive or linguistic response to a story or poem; we can work through feelings and sensory perception. We can simplify, by adapting the language to the level of the individual – telling stories in simple short sentences, or even sequences of single words. At the same time, we can enrich the text by creating sensory associations through tone of voice, visual and sound effects, which add contextual meaning. Some units of text can be provided as complete scripts, without needing to paraphrase, and treated like stretches of atmospheric music. In the next chapter, we will look in detail at the structure of stories, plays and poetry, and their adaptation for students with difficulties in language and learning.

CHAPTER 4

Adapting stories, plays and poetry: working principles

> I'll tell you a story
> About Jackanory
> And now my story's begun.
> I'll tell you another
> About John his brother
> And now my story is done.
>
> **Traditional**

> Faint brief cry and immediately inspiration and slow increase of light together reaching maximum together in about ten seconds. Silence and hold about five seconds.
>
> Expiration and slow decrease of light together reaching minimum together...in about ten seconds and immediately cry as before. Silence and hold about five seconds.
>
> **Samuel Beckett** *Breath*

Principles of adaptation

Making decisions about the adaptation of texts for any presentation involves having a clear sense of the nature of the audience, the purpose of the presentation, and the nature of the text. In seeking to adapt works of literature, we need to clarify the answers to some simple questions: what? why? who for? and how? We need to choose a text (*what?*) and have a clear purpose in mind (*why?*) for a particular audience (*who for?*), and we need to know how we are going to present it. The preceding chapters have argued for a set of fundamental 'ground rules' which we can use to develop guidelines for adaptation.

In answer to the *What?* question, we have established that in this context 'anything goes'; any text, that is, which excites you enough to want to share it – any text that interests students. We would also concur with the authors of the Cox report that we want students to have some knowledge of the best stories, plays and poetry around, reflecting a variety of cultures and styles.

Our answer to the *Why?* question differs radically from the stated purpose of literature within the English curriculum. We certainly do want as many of our students as possible to become effective readers – but our purpose in providing them with experiences of stories, plays and poetry has little to do with functional literacy, and more to do with developing imagination, empathy, engagement, self-expression and shared knowledge of texts. This means that we can look beyond print as a means of access when we come to consider the *How?* question.

The audience we have in mind in this book are students with difficulties in language and learning. The linguistic perspective has provided insights into the nature of comprehension which suggest that we can compensate for these difficulties in two ways – by simplifying and by enriching experiences. The high level of sensory impairments associated with some special educational needs is also a factor which must be considered when adapting texts: for students with visual and/or hearing difficulties, it is not enough to read a story or use pictures to tell it. The guiding principle for this audience is that of 'partial participation' – that students should be given the opportunity to take part in experiences that are deemed to be of value, at whatever level is appropriate for them.

In answer to the *How?* question, we have suggested that all forms of media are relevant to sharing literature with students; performance, music and pictorial illustrations can be amplified with other sensory associations – smells, tastes and tactile stimuli. Alternative forms of communication and writing need to be used where appropriate.

The guiding principles which underpin the approach to adaptation in this book can therefore be summarised as follows:

- Literature nourishes the development of feeling and imagination, as well as of the critical faculties. Affect and engagement are central to response to literature.
- Access to literature is not dependent on access to literacy. Drama and multisensory presentations are legitimate routes to the experience of stories, drama and poetry. Manual signs and symbol systems should be used alongside speech to convey meaning.
- We can enable students to experience something of the essence of a text, even if they cannot grasp everything.
- Apprehending involves more than comprehending. Students who cannot decode meaning may be able to apprehend meaning through repeated associations and inference.

With these principles in mind, this chapter focuses in more detail on the questions of *What?* and *How?* – what is the nature of a particular work of literature, and how can it be presented to students across the range of ability.

Structural frameworks – looking at texts

Current literary theories emphasise the active role of the reader in the construction of a text (see Peach and Burton 1995). A work of literature only comes alive in the mind of its audience, whose understanding of its meaning is filtered through the life experiences of each individual. In this sense, every text is realised in a thousand different ways. My *Romeo and Juliet* will not be quite the same as yours. Sharing stories, plays or poems with an audience always involves an interpretation, and interpretations become adaptations when aspects of the original are changed or selectively heightened. For students with special educational needs, we are always likely to be engaged in the adaptation of texts – and for this we need make no apology. However, we do need to know what we are changing, and why we are doing it. So, let us look at the construction of text, taking the novel as the basic form.

If you tell a friend that you have just read a new novel, one of the first questions they are likely to ask is: 'What's it about?' If you try to answer that question in any detail, you will probably find yourself saying something about the type of book (e.g. a crime story or a romance), the main message, something about the plot, something about the people in the book and something about its atmosphere. You might also mention the style of the writing, if it is sufficiently striking to you. These are the basic elements which go into the pot and come out as the story you have read. Some elements may be more prominent than others. In many thrillers, for example, plot is emphasised at the expense of character. Analysing how these elements combine in particular texts provides a way in to developing an adaptation (see Figure 4.1).

Theme
Genre
Narrative
Character
Scene
Language

Figure 4.1 *Elements of literature*

Theme

The theme of the work is its driving force: the central issue which the author seems to want to convey. There may be more than one theme, and particular chapters, verses or scenes may have their own themes. By deciding on what you see as the main theme, you can anchor the presentation of the text. Theme is related to genre.

Genre

This is a term denoting the conventions within which the work will be framed. Particular genres have associated traditions which set up expectations in the minds of the audience or readers. The Player King in Tom Stoppard's *Rosencrantz and Guildenstern are Dead* explains the rules which govern his choice of productions:

> I can do you blood and love without the rhetoric, and I can do you blood and rhetoric without the love, and I can do you all three concurrent or consecutive, but I can't do you love and rhetoric without the blood. Blood is compulsory... (Act I)

These traditions can of course be subverted – as they are in *Whose Line is it Anyway?*, the television game where players are required to act out banal scenes in particular styles (for example, selling dusters in Hammer Horror mode). Some texts do not conform to any genre in particular, but using conventions can help to establish the atmosphere and tone of what you do. For example, there are typical kinds of music associated with chase, murder, knockabout comedy and love, which you can use to bring a sense of coherence to activities. Deciding on theme and genre is a good starting point for working on a text. If you know what the theme is going to be, you can start to think about how the other elements of the text will be selected and combined to convey what you want to get across.

Narrative

The plot or story line is the path along which the work travels. Narrative has been described as a 'primary act of mind' (Hardy 1975), in that our lives are an unfolding tale with a defined beginning and end, and we seem to have an unquenchable appetite for turning our experiences into story form. At its most basic, a story line involves an event with a start point and an end point, as the traditional rhyme at the beginning of this chapter suggests. Beckett's *Breath* suggests that the start and the end are all that is important – and these are universal. Narrative is driven by action and consequence, which link the event to character through motive. Some students may not be able to follow a plot as such, but they will be sensitive to the signals that open and close events in their daily lives. This awareness can be exploited in symbolic form in the presentation of narratives. For students with learning difficulties, the best narratives to use are those with a strong, explicit and logical story line which can be simplified without too much omission or distortion of the original.

Character

The imaginary people in a story are brought to life by the author's ability to create impressions which are vivid and real, and feelings and responses to the plot which engage our interest. Exploration of character typically involves analysing motive and reaction, and the relationship between the nature of the person and the way it is conveyed through the roles taken in the story, what they say, and how they are described. However, a sense of character can be gained by quite small characteristics. Peggy Ashcroft used to say that she always started with the shoes, in building up her characters for the stage. In a workshop for teachers, we had a lot of fun planning how to portray one of Thomas Hardy's characters through smell. For students with learning difficulties, the best characters are those who can be easily identified and contrasted, who lend themselves to role play, and where feeling and motive can be readily deduced from behaviour within the narrative. For example, characters whose speech patterns and actions are highly distinctive; characters who are described in very visual terms.

Scene

The scene of a work is the context in which it takes place, which also sets its atmospheric tone. By exploring the scene, you create the backdrop for the plot and characters. Explicit information about scene is provided by the stage directions in a play, or descriptions of setting in a novel. Developing atmosphere offers enormous potential for conveying something of the essence of a text to people who have difficulties understanding language. For students with learning difficulties, look for strongly atmospheric and contrastive scenes, which lend themselves to illustration through sensory effects – art, colour, music and sounds, textures, smells.

Language

The language of poetry, plays and novels presents the biggest stumbling block to teachers attempting to share literature with students who have learning difficulties. The problem is complex because once the language is changed, we are in danger of losing the core of the work. You can retell and simplify the story of a Shakespeare play, but if you use none of the original text, are you offering students anything of any value?

It was argued in the previous chapter that this problem can be addressed by using two routes to the use of language: 'bottom-up' and 'top-down'. A second principle which is helpful is that of partial participation: that is, you may not be able to use the whole text, but you should be able to use extracts. Even the most complex texts will have some passages which are written simply enough to be used directly.

Accessible language styles seem to have the following characteristics:

Simplicity

Simple sentence construction and basic vocabulary. A good test of the clarity of the language is the ease with which you can sign it or translate it into graphic symbols.

Concreteness

Descriptive language referring to sensory experiences which can be illustrated by real examples or pictures.

Rhythm and sound

Language which is strongly patterned, conveying meaning through sound and sense. Onomatopoeia is the technical term for words with in-built sound effects (e.g. 'moo', 'splat', 'tee-hee', 'pitter-patter'). This language can be readily illustrated by sounds or music, using contrasts between vowels and consonants; short sounds and long sounds; hard sounds and soft sounds.

Repetition

Language which builds up meaning through repeated sequences and refrains (e.g. traditional folk and fairy tales, songs and ballads).

Dramatic language

Language which conveys character, or narrative, and can be illustrated through acting, exaggerated for emphasis.

Appendix 1 provides some examples of poetry which illustrate these aspects of language.

Choosing texts

In adapting texts for students with special educational needs, you can play around with the elements of narrative, character, scene and language. For students with profound learning difficulties, you might emphasise the contrasting atmospheres, or scenes, of different events in the text, whereas for other students you might want to focus on the story line, developing their abilities to predict and reason. You do not have to work on all elements at once, or even at all. Figure 4.2 offers a simple planning framework for looking at these elements in the text you select.

Theme and Genre What do you see as the main theme or point of the text? Does it fall into a particular genre? e.g. heroic epic; thriller; romance; comedy; tragedy; soap opera.
Narrative Summarise the main story line. What events will you include? Brainstorm some ideas for conveying the story line to students.
Character Who are the main characters? Who are the minor characters? Which characters do you plan to include? Choose one or two adjectives to characterise each one.
Scene What scenes or moods provide the setting for the main events? Brainstorm some ideas for conveying atmosphere.
Language Choose some extracts from the text that are: • relatively simple, direct language that could be understood by some of your students; • evocative, descriptive language that could be enriched with sensory association; • rhythmic, patterned language that you could move to, or use like a piece of music; • very well known; • important to story line or character.
Primary focus What will your primary focus be in this adaptation? *Narrative* *Character* *Scene* *Language*

Figure 4.2 *Planning framework for stories, plays, poems*

You will find, in looking at literature, that these elements are not always present in equal measure. For example, take this poem by Thomas Wyatt:

> I promised you
> And you promised me
> To be as true
> As I would be.
> But since I see
> Your double heart
> Farewell my part!

Lyrics like this are designed to express directly the feelings of the poet. There is no narrative, nor character. The components are language and mood (which is, if you like, the internalised 'scene' or context).

Or take Dickens' *Pickwick Papers*. Here we have a very vivid cast of characters, exuberant language and a clearly defined scene, but far less emphasis on narrative than in his other novels. By contrast, a thriller such as *Day of the Jackal* offers us an engrossing narrative, but little character interest.

When you are choosing a novel, play or poem to use with students, you should also bear in mind the following criteria:

Cultural significance to individuals or communities

- works which have had a lasting influence on the development of literature;
- images, events and characters which have popular recognition and lead to shared experiences;
- works which are relevant to students' current experiences.

Familiar extracts and cliches are indicators that a work has cultural significance. Even if your pupils only grasp one line, knowing 'Romeo, Romeo, wherefore art thou Romeo' gives them a toehold in the wider community. Catchphrases are likely to get reinforced, even if only through advertisements.

Film and tv versions

It is an advantage if the text you want to use is available on film. Beware of simplified animated versions – although these can be useful as summaries of the story, they may not actually hold pupils' attention. Particularly if you are exploring feelings, motives and reactions, real actors are much better, although you may have to be selective and use extracts, filling in the story line yourself.

Your favourites!

This is the most important principle of all. If you really like a text, you will find a way to share it.

Having chosen a particular text, and developed the basic approach, we move to exploring in more detail ways of handling the language, using the model derived from the discussion of comprehension and expression.

In Chapter 3 it was suggested that two approaches to conveying meaning can operate in parallel: simplification, and enrichment. Figure 4.3 illustrates the features of each approach.

Adapting language – simplification and enrichment

Simplify text **(Decode model)**
Bottom-up One word -> 2 words -> 3 words -> 4 words -> Complex language *Bring the child to the text*

Enrich text **(Inferential model)**
Top-down Sound and rhythm of language + Rich associations + Scripts *Bring the text to the child*

Figure 4.3 Two approaches to meaning

Simplification

In the first approach, we start with the child. The principle involves providing input at a level appropriate to the child's ability to decode language, simplifying or explaining vocabulary, and making few assumptions about what the child may be using from the context. Using the terminology of the *Derbyshire Language Scheme* (Knowles and Masidlover 1982), we build up from one 'information carrying' word, to two words, to three words, to four words, and thence to 'grammar and complex language'.

As soon as we look at a complex text, it becomes apparent that this approach will be inadequate if we want to provide children with real experiences of literature. Take, for example, the following speech from *Macbeth*.

> Now o'er the one half world
> Nature seems dead, and wicked dreams abuse
> The curtain'd sleep. Witchcraft celebrates
> Pale Hecate's offerings, and withered murder
> Alarumed by his sentinel, the wolf,
> Whose howl's his watch, thus with his stealthy pace
> With Tarquin's ravishing strides, towards his design
> Moves like a ghost. Thou sure and firm-set earth
> Hear not my steps, which way they walk, for fear
> The very stones prate of my whereabouts
> And take the present horror from the time
> Which now suits with it. Whiles I threat, he lives
> Words to the heat of deeds too cold breath gives.

Macbeth (II:i: 49-61)

On the face of it, this passage is fraught with difficulty if you want to use it with students who have difficulties in language and learning. The syntax is complex (try to sort out the pronominal referents for 'his' in lines 53–55, or the subjects of the verbs in lines 58–59). There are numerous impenetrable classical allusions. The language is archaic, and worse, when we do recognise a word (such as 'watch', 'present', 'suits') the meaning is likely to be quite other than that which first occurs to us. If we try to paraphrase the speech, we come up with something so banal, we wish we had never started: 'It is night and everything is quiet. Witches, wolves and ghosts prowl around . . . Earth – do not listen to my steps. While I stand here talking, he goes on living. The more I talk, the more my desire to act grows cold . . .'

What happens if we try the second approach?

Enrichment

Here we start with the text and explore its atmosphere, meaning and sound. Instead of working with the literal, surface form and decoding it into a simpler version, we have to consider the sub-text, the context, and the impact of allusions, and translate these into sensory associations which can illustrate and embody the feeling in which the text is grounded. We use the sound and rhythm of language, and whole phrases, which function as 'scripts' associated with particular events. This is a 'top-down' approach which actively exploits context to create experiences and to bring the text to the child.

In the case of the *Macbeth* speech, we might ask the following questions:

- How does the sound of the text relate to its meaning?
- What images and associations are called up by the text?
- Which parts of the text work as whole scripts?

If you read the text aloud, and try moving to its rhythms, you will see how much of it is written in half lines. The sense trips over from one line to the next, in a way which mirrors Macbeth's fearful, jerky thoughts. If we take 'hear not my steps' as the basis for working with the text, we can move first in one direction, then another, then stop, then start again (you can, of course, push a wheelchair in this rhythm). Using our voices, we find that, although there are only four sentences, it's difficult to produce the speech with only four pauses. If we take our breaths at the commas, after each phrase, we immediately get a sense of gasping panic. We have now got a long way into feeling what the passage tells us, without any decoding at all. If we next think about the images, they are associated with darkness and death (the 'cold breath' of line 61 is a dramatic irony). So we might darken the room, creating a shadow on a backcloth with light or torch, and introduce the occasional scary noise (a wolf howl, the sounds of our steps). Finally, scripts. Having read the whole speech to the group and encouraged them to move and vocalise through it, we could separate sections to be programmed onto speech output devices, activated by switches. Macbeth shifts the psychological perspective from external to internal in this speech; first he is the observer of the night, then a partner in a dialogue, then he reflects on himself and his actions. Each perspective can be taken by a different student.

Enriching texts does not preclude simplifying them. Once students have made the emotional connections with the speech, it is possible to go back to it, translate, and help them to decode meanings. The difference is, though, that you are giving them the whole experience and adding in the simpler meanings, not stripping the text of its resonance, and leaving them with the bare bones of the paraphrase. For this reason, it is vital to go back to the original text for your inspiration, rather than relying on simplified versions, which do not have the rich symbolic significance which you will need to adapt in a way that is faithful and not tokenistic. For example, when we were working on *Far from the Madding Crowd* (see below) in a workshop, one teacher realised that although the film uses a wide open space as the context for Troy's seduction of Bathsheba, the original location is enclosed and secret. This provided a starting point for thinking about how to create the atmosphere with pupils with profound learning difficulties. If you work only from a story version of *Romeo and Juliet*, you will miss the hand to hand contact described in the sonnet of their first exchange, which would allow you to dramatise the relationship in a relevant tactile way for pupils with sensory impairments.

Applying the framework: Far from the Madding Crowd

Thomas Hardy is one of the authors recommended for study at Key Stage 3, and *Far from the Madding Crowd* is one of his most accessible books. It is highly atmospheric, set in rural Dorset through changing seasons and with many references to contemporary folk songs and dances, which can be used to provide musical illustrations. The characters and the story line can be simplified without too much distortion and the themes of love and loss are archetypal in their appeal. The genre is essentially romantic fiction.

Plot summary

Gabriel Oak is a shepherd who loves the beautiful but headstrong Bathsheba Everdene. When he loses all his flock in an accident, he goes to work for her at her farm. Bathsheba is courted by her rich neighbour, Farmer Boldwood, but she falls for Sergeant Troy, a handsome ne'er do well, and marries him. Troy has already seduced her maid, Fanny, who dies in childbirth. He disappears, but re-enters Bathsheba's life just as she is about to marry Boldwood. Boldwood shoots Troy and goes to prison, and Bathsheba realises that, after all, Gabriel is the man for her.

Characters

Gabriel: strong, patient, trustworthy
Bathsheba: beautiful, proud
Troy: handsome, faithless, greedy
Boldwood: silent, serious, rich
Fanny: sad, poor

Troy seduces Bathsheba

Troy and Bathsheba meet in an enclosed green dell, where he entertains her with a display of sword drill. Bathsheba stands firm as his sword flashes around her – 'don't you trust me not to hurt you?' he asks. Of course, we know that Troy is actually a bounder and a cad, who is after her money, and will break her heart. At the end of the scene, they embrace.

The main emphasis in this episode is on atmosphere and character relationships rather than narrative, although when we are tracing the overall story line, this scene is pivotal.

Themes: Trust and betrayal
             Passion

Characters:
Bathsheba (white, flower scent: innocence, beauty)
Troy (red, tacky aftershave, gold chains on hairy chest: army, danger, passion)

Language: Extracts from the dialogue: *Stand still; Are you sure you won't hurt me?; Quite sure; One, two, three, four; Is the sword sharp?; Oh no! ; I must be leaving you.*

Scene: A green, enclosed, quiet space. Use dappled or green lighting, birdsong, gentle wind as the background.

Activities:
Sword drill: Using light beams, torches or silver foil swords, the students take it in turns to act Troy and Bathsheba in the centre of a circle.

The kiss: Use red and white streamers intertwined to link Troy and Bathsheba together. This is an echo of the way Troy winds a lock of her hair around his finger as a keepsake.

Trust: With those students who are able, enact the theme of betrayal by playing tricks. For example, the game where a person is shown obstacles around the room, then blindfolded and led around the course – but in the meantime, all the obstacles have been removed. The partner is actually tricking them and betraying their trust.

The storm

On Troy and Bathsheba's wedding night, there is a dance for all the farmhands. Troy gets the men drunk, and refuses to come out when Gabriel warns him that there will be a storm, and that they should set to to cover the hay ricks. The emphasis here is more on the narrative – the conflict.

Themes: Conflict; storm

Narrative: Gabriel pleads with Troy and his friends to come out and help him. They refuse.

Characters: Gabriel (wants to work). Troy (wants to play).

Activities:
Conflict: dramatise this with a tug of war. Start with Troy and Gabriel on opposite ends. Other students join in on one or other side, using lines from the episode such as: *Protect the ricks/hay; It will not rain; A heavy rain will fall; We'll enjoy ourselves;*
At the end of the tug of war, Troy's followers win, and they fall back on the floor in a 'drunken stupor'.

The storm: Use musical instruments, tapping on backs or drumming on the floor, water sprays, to build up the storm. At its height, there should be thunder, lightning and driving rain.
Build a 'rick' with chairs and wedges. Two pupils try to cover it with a large sheet, while blown on and rained on by the storm.

Language: Dialogue from the scene (see below). Phrases which refer to the storm, e.g. *The lightning was the colour of silver, and gleamed in the heavens; Rumbles became rattles; All was silent, and black as a cave; From every part of the tumbling sky there came a shout.*

Scene: Contrast between indoors (the barn) which is safe and warm and full of light, laughter and dance music, with the outside, dark and wet and dangerous, with storm noises.

Summary

This chapter has presented some working principles for adapting stories, plays and poetry. The next chapters will present some examples from teachers and therapists who are using literature in their work.

CHAPTER 5

Literature in the classroom: from principles to practice

> But all the children
> are listening to the music
> and the walls of the classroom
> quietly crumble
> The windowpanes turn
> once more to sand
> the ink is sea
> the desk is trees
> the chalk is cliffs
> and the quill pen
> a bird again.
>
> **Paul Dehn** *Exercise Book* (translated from Jacques Prevert)

Philosophies and principles offer starting points, but translating these into practice in the classroom can seem a daunting task, faced with all the pressures of time, staff shortages, limited resources and the inevitable emergencies. A more serious problem is posed by the sheer diversity of difficulties in language and communication, which means that approaches which will work brilliantly with some students will fall totally flat with others. Teachers need to become rather like magicians, weaving different spells from the same ingredients to open all those different doors to the world of imagination. This chapter begins with summaries of the main difficulties in language and learning for students with moderate/severe learning difficulties, autism, specific language impairment, deafness and profound and multiple learning difficulties. Some relevant practical strategies are suggested under each heading, but this should not be taken to mean that they can only be used with students who have these specific difficulties, since many of the techniques have been found to be helpful across the board. Next, some examples of projects are provided from schools for pupils with learning difficulties, specific language difficulties and autism. The chapter ends with some ideas for illustration, and some well-tried approaches from drama and English teaching for engaging with texts.

Teaching strategies for problems in language and learning

Moderate/severe learning difficulties

The term 'learning difficulties' is a general description relating to problems in adaptive functioning, ranging from mild to moderate, severe and profound. In the ability range of severe to profound learning difficulties, cognitive and linguistic impairments are likely to have an organic cause, resulting in damage to the developing brain. The precise nature of the learning difficulty will vary depending on the pattern of what has been affected and what has been relatively spared, and on the kind of experiences and opportunities to learn which the child has been afforded in life. There may be associated impairments to vision, hearing or motor skills, a high incidence of medical problems such as epilepsy (Kelleher and Mulcahey 1986) and psychological disturbances such as autism, and specific language difficulties.

As a broad generalisation, students with severe learning difficulties are likely to have short attention spans, find it hard to remember information and generalise from one context to another, and to handle abstract concepts. They will find it easier to understand language which is associated with everyday, meaningful events than language which is abstract and de-contextualised; easier to process information which is given in short chunks, and which is repeated consistently. They may become confused when bombarded with too much information at a time. Expressive language tends not to develop much beyond the level of simple sentences, with many students using only one or two words to communicate at a time. Vocabularies are dominated by concrete, familiar terms, with a high ratio of nouns to verbs and other parts of speech. Severe speech impairments are common, leading to the use of augmentative and alternative communication systems such as manual signs or gestures, books and aids with pictures or graphic symbols. In conversation, students with severe learning difficulties often find it hard to initiate and maintain turns, or to understand the different ways in which language is adapted and used in social situations. At a personal level, students with severe learning difficulties who do not have additional emotional/behavioural problems, form close and loving relationships, and can understand and express a full range of feelings from humour and enjoyment to intense sadness. Many students will be able to play symbolically and enjoy drama and role play, but for others, there should be no demand to pretend. Instead, as suggested by Heathcote (1984), students should be provided with a clearly defined real experience to which they only have to *respond*.

These common patterns of learning difficulties suggest that successful strategies for using literature with this group of pupils will involve:

- Use of sensory cues to gain attention, aid memory and establish atmosphere (smell, taste, touch, sight and sound).
- Structured presentation of information (sensory cues must not be overwhelming).
- Relatively short sessions (or sessions broken up into short episodes).
- Listening reinforced by doing. For example, teach a catch phrase or an action which can be done by the whole group at certain points in the story. Find elements that can be acted, or mimed or dramatised by grouping the students.
- Extensive preparation. Tell students something of what the story is about and who the characters are before you start. Have pictures and props ready so that the story can be illustrated.
- Repetition. Stories become familiar and accrue meaning through repeated experience. This allows students to build up a network of associations, and will make it easier for them to anticipate what is happening and to participate. Once the overall framework is familiar, you can vary elements within it to maintain interest and attention.
- A story can gradually be assembled by 'layering'. Break it down into small episodes, complete in themselves, and start each week by repeating an earlier episode or 'layer' until the students are thoroughly familiar with it.

- An alternative strategy is to start with a complete, but very simple, outline of the story, familiarise the students with this, and then gradually build in elaboration.
- Very clear transitions between one event and the next.
- Emphasis on the affective, feeling aspects of the text (top-down approach).
- Simplifications of character and story line. Be ruthless in cutting out elements which are irrelevant to your main theme, or which are too complex.
- Visual story line. Put the story line on a wall display, with scenes clearly outlined and linked with arrows. Establish where you are each time.
- Character types. Establish simple character types. In many dramas and stories there are 'stock' characters such as the lovers, the villain, the clown, and you can often slot characters into these roles. Give each character an identifying feature, such as a prop, or a sign.
- Character maps. Character maps are visual displays which show the links between characters, or their roles in the story: e.g. 'good' vs. 'bad' characters.
- Opportunities to generalise their understanding of the story through associated activities in other areas of the curriculum such as art and music.
- Programming lines from stories or poems onto simple switch operated communication aids, or language masters. Any story or poem with a repetitive refrain offers a good starting point, for example:

I'll huff and I'll puff and I'll blow your house down (*Three Little Pigs*)

And still she sat, and still she reeled, and still she wished for company
(*The Strange Guest*, Scottish traditional poem)

Far and few, far and few
Are the lands where the Jumblies live
Their heads are green and their hands are blue
And they went to sea in a sieve
(Edward Lear, *The Jumblies*)

'What saw thou there?' said the King
'Sir, I saw nothing but the waters wap and the waves wan'
(Thomas Malory, *The Death of Arthur*)

Repeated refrains can be used in stories and plays as well, for example when characters appear, or at the beginning or end of the session.

Autistic spectrum

Autism used to be thought of as a unitary disorder, but it is now more generally recognised as a spectrum or continuum of particular features which can affect individuals right across the range of ability. The primary difficulty appears to lie in the area of social cognition, which means that autistic children find it hard to see the world from the point of view of others and to interpret emotions and social behaviour. Their interactions tend to be instrumental (getting things done for me) rather than motivated by the desire to share information and feelings with others. It has been suggested that the failure to engage with other people underlies the other problems commonly associated with autism, such as an over-literal understanding, difficulties with symbolic play and ritualistic obsessions (Hobson 1993). According to this argument, people with autism can relate to the world of things, and do not necessarily have problems understanding means – end relations such as tool use, or the substitution of one set of features for another. Thus some individuals can engage in a limited form of symbolic play (making a matchbox into a car, for example). However, they find it much harder to take on roles, or understand the symbolic meanings related to others' experience (Jordan and Libby 1997).

Individuals at the more severe end of the autistic continuum may fail to develop any language, or use only a few words or signs, often imitated rather than spontaneous. Other individuals may develop language to an advanced level in some respects. Typically pronunciation and grammar are intact and sophisticated, and the main problems are to do with pragmatics, or the social use of language. Because their understanding tends to be very literal, autistic people find it hard to discern double meanings such as sarcasm, jokes or metaphorical use of language. Their difficulties with determining what will be relevant for another person to know mean that they are likely to be over specific in their answers (telling you far more about what they did yesterday than you want to know) or under specific (answering 'yes' when asked at the door if mummy is at home).

Recent research on word meanings suggests that although autistic children may develop very similar vocabularies to non-autistic children, they may use and understand words in rather idiosyncratic ways (Tager-Flusberg 1993). In particular, they have a limited understanding and use of terms to do with feelings and mental states (thinking, believing, knowing, imagining etc.). The story narratives of autistic people tend to be somewhat mechanistic – they may be able to describe what happened, but not what it meant to the participants (Loveland and Tunali 1993). However, autistic people may have some areas of strength in language. They may have good rote memories for lines of poetry and enjoy the sound of words in rhymes and nonsense verse. They may also like word play and word associations. Where personal relationships are concerned, the classic descriptions of autism suggest an incapacity to feel or form bonds. However, more recent insights suggest that autistic individuals may be attached to their families, and long to form friendships, but lack the knowledge and skills of how to do so appropriately, or how to show their feelings (Hobson 1993; Rumsey, Rapoport and Sceery 1985).

The characteristics associated with autism suggest that there will be certain aspects of literature that these students will find difficult, particularly in the interplay of character and narrative. Whilst they may be able to follow a story, it will be very hard for them to interpret motivation and predict consequences, or to empathise imaginatively with what is going on. Approaches to literature which start by creating an emotional atmosphere may be less effective with this group of students than approaches which emphasise explicit logical patterns, and the sound and rhythms of words. It is important to be sensitive to obsessions – some students may have idiosyncratic phobias or fads which you may need to take account of in planning. For example, if you are doing *Macbeth* and one of the students has a real thing about knives, you might choose to avoid the daggers, or use very crude cardboard shapes.

Despite the difficulties, literature offers a rich source of opportunities for working directly on some of the social skills which are needed by these students.

Most of the strategies which have been suggested for pupils with learning disabilities will be relevant for students with autistic spectrum disorders. In addition, successful strategies include:

- Making things explicit. Bring out the motivation of characters, and explain the difference between what people think, what people feel and how they behave. Picture symbols can be used to put next to characters, which state how they are feeling: sad, worried, happy etc.
- Exaggerated displays of emotion, so that students can see the contrasts clearly.
- Providing scripts that enable students to rehearse pretend events. For example, photographs of key events in a drama, which students sequence to 'unfold' the story, which they then re-enact (Jordan and Libby 1997).
- Cues to structure discussion about the text. For example, a cue to stop the action or the storytelling (such as a fake remote control) followed by standard questions such as 'what's going to happen next?' 'why did s/he do that?'
- Translating the story or drama into a board game that has clear formal rules (see Figure 5.1). Logical games may help pupils to access the events (Jordan and Libby 1997).
- Cues which help students to understand key features of narratives, character or scene.
  Images traditionally associated with the countryside or city, which at one level may be cliches, can help autistic children to fix on something essential. Graphic devices such as thought bubbles compared to speech bubbles and a heart shaped bubble for feeling. Large question marks or exclamation marks. (See Figure 5.2.)
  Sound cues such as scary music, chase music, or the rippling scales that always indicate a flash back in time.
- Games and tasks to explore metaphor and figurative language: for example, visual similarities between objects.
- A consistent structure in your presentations, so that students become familiar with a way to approach and understand stories, for example, routines to begin and end a session.

The principle of the board game translates achievements into advances along the board, and disasters into delays or reversals.

E.g. You have fallen into the Slough of Despond. Miss a turn.

You have left your scroll half way down the Hill of Difficulty. Go back three spaces to retrieve it.

You are now in the Palace Beautiful. Have a second go.

The game can also be used to explore motivation and character, by predicting whether the people the Pilgrims encounter will be friends or foes. For example, you might turn up character cards, and guess – if you are correct, you move on a space.

Mr. Worldly Wise says he knows how to help you, just follow him along this easy path. Will you go or not?

You have landed in the castle grounds of Giant Despair. Do you think it would be a good idea to ask if you can stay the night?

Figure 5.1 Suggestions for a Pilgrim's Progress board game

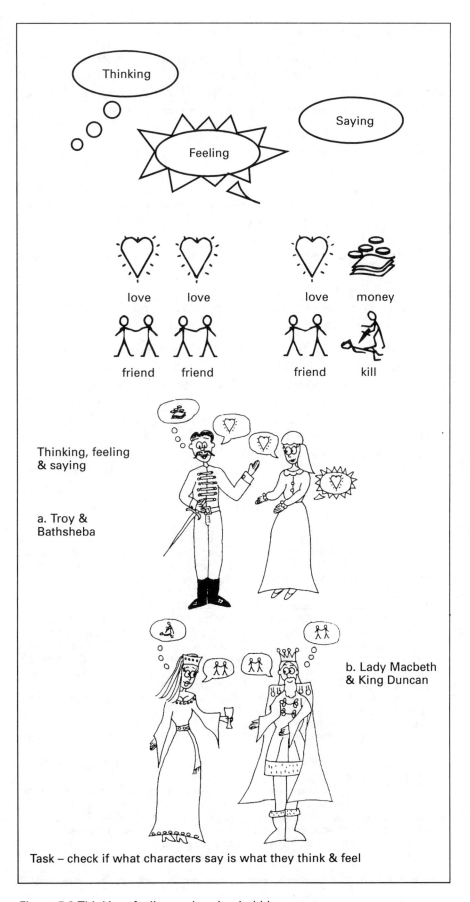

Figure 5.2 Thinking, feeling and saying bubbles

Specific language impairments

If students have particular problems with understanding or expressive language, over and above what would be expected from their levels of achievement in other areas of learning, they are described as having a specific language impairment. One or more of the following aspects of language may be affected:

- *vocabulary and word meanings*
  difficulties with finding the right word, or understanding the range of meanings of a word.
- *grammar*
  difficulties with constructing well formed utterances: grammatical elements may be left out, or put in the wrong places.
- *pronunciation*
  difficulties with producing, and possibly perceiving, speech sounds, so that speech is hard to understand.
- *social use of language*
  the child may use language inappropriately, and finds difficulty in managing both verbal and nonverbal aspects of conversation.

Expressive language is often more severely affected than comprehension, but recent research, reviewed by Bishop (1997), suggests that there are nearly always some problems with understanding, although these may not be apparent in everyday conversation where there are many contextual cues. For example, the child may find stories difficult to interpret because of the several demands on attention and on the ability to make inferences and to integrate information into a cohesive whole. Bishop suggests that some of the techniques which have been used to help poor readers understand written texts could be applied to oral comprehension (Oakhill 1994) (see Figure 5.3). Other text-based approaches to develop reading skills can be found in Lunzer and Gardner (1984).

- Encourage students to verbalise and explain their own experiences.
- Teach inferential skills explicitly by focusing on 'cue words' that allow you to infer missing information – for example 'Tom was shivering on the doorstep, waiting for his mum to come home.' What does each word tell us? e.g. Tom is a boy; he is cold; he wants to get into a house, the house is his; he does not have a key, but he thinks his mother does.
- Teach explicit use of different types of questions: for literal information, interpretations (e.g. of character and intention); inferences (what is implied from the words in the text) and evaluations (what views can be taken about the meaning, the message or the appeal of the story). Encourage students to develop their own scripted questions to ask one another (e.g. using a TV interview format).
- Use who, what, why, when, how questions to generate information, first for sentences, then for paragraphs, then for stories.
- Teach skills of summary and paraphrase, focusing on the main ideas in the text (e.g. by highlighting important words or sections in different colours).
- Omit relevant sections from a story, and encourage pupils to work out what is missing.
- Mental imagery. From the age of about eight years, deliberate evocation of mental pictures (e.g. to depict the main event, or a sequence of events) can help with text comprehension. The first step is to provide an illustration which students are asked to recall when describing the story, then to encourage students to visualise their own pictures.

Figure 5.3 *Strategies for developing comprehension of texts (based on Oakhill 1994)*

The understanding of non-literal language is often supposed to present a difficulty to children with specific language impairments. However, investigations of idiom comprehension suggest that the problem may lie more in the area of pragmatics (knowing when it is appropriate to infer idiomatic usage) than in difficulties with understanding the meaning of the idiom itself (Kerbel and Grunwell 1998a). To use one example provided by the authors, a child may be able to correctly point to a picture which indicates happiness when he hears the expression 'full of beans' but interpret it literally in context, because he does not have an expectation of idiomatic language in a particular social situation. Research methodology from various projects suggests that some children who are unable to provide definitions of idioms can successfully identify figurative over literal meaning in a picture selection task, or act out idioms in a play task (Kerbel and Grunwell 1998a, b; Vance and Wells 1994).

For students whose main problems are in the area of learning, recalling and interpreting *vocabulary* it may be helpful to:

- Explain words with difficult meanings by giving a simpler equivalent that is within the student's vocabulary (bottom-up approach).
- Emphasise the affective and rhythmic aspects of unfamiliar text, to build up a sense of the meaning (top-down approach).
- Focus on the words that the student really needs to know in order to grasp the meaning (for example, names of characters and places) and de-emphasise complex words which are less relevant.
- Use riddles and descriptive poetry which can provide useful opportunities for building up associations and getting students to attend to and retrieve word meanings.
- Use word substitution games, similes and metaphors which offer ways of helping students to build up networks of meaning and simultaneously explore the meaning of a text.
- Use quotations from the text to build up a foundation to aid comprehension of the whole text.

Additionally, for students whose main problems are in the area of *grammar*:

- Use colour to highlight parts of speech.

Students whose problems are in word *pronunciation* may find it difficult to recognise complex or unfamiliar words, and will find any oral recitation a challenge.

- They can be encouraged to put speeches into their own words, to mime or gesture difficult passages, use tape recordings or communication aids with their own voices or those of others; join in group recitals with one well chosen word or phrase.
- Working on the rhythm and intonation of a piece, without worrying too much about the exact pronunciation of individual words, will help their intelligibility.

Students who have problems with the *social use of language* can be helped by the same approaches which have been suggested for autistic spectrum disorders.

Deafness and dual sensory impairments

Many individuals with severe hearing impairments do not get sufficient input in a comprehensible form during the critical period of language acquisition, and are left with difficulties in understanding complex language. This presents particular problems in the area of literature, especially if in addition, the student has a learning difficulty. In addition to the strategies outlined above, it is obviously necessary to present information visually and through movement. This might include:

- clear pictorial illustrations;
- visual plot line;
- maps of relationships between characters;
- collages of scenes, with emblematic use of colour (e.g. red for love, passion, anger; black for grief; yellow for happiness etc.).

Mime, gesture and sign offer obvious routes to meaning, but care should be taken in translation. As with any other language, a pedantic emphasis on word for word rendition is more likely to obscure the sense of a passage than to clarify it. There are similar issues involved in translation from text to graphic symbols such as Rebus (Detheridge and Detheridge 1997). Sign has its own visual logic, which is exploited in its poetry. Principles for translation from spoken to sign language, and from text to symbols, can be found in Appendix 2.

- For students who are deaf and have a learning difficulty, it is probably best to use one or two key signs, rather than attempt to render a complete story or poem in sign.
- Dance and movement offer creative routes to meaning for deaf students – try exploring ways of moving to the rhythm of a poem, or conveying its meaning through visual images.

Dual sensory impairments and profound learning difficulties

People with profound and multiple learning difficulties may have both visual and auditory impairments. They will be relying on the proximal senses of touch, taste and smell to gain information about the world, and need to be given plenty of space and time to understand what is happening. Because students may have unpredictable responses to sensory stimuli, such as tactile-defensiveness, it is important to base your planning for their involvement on individual needs and preferences. *Odyssey Now* (Grove and Park 1996) was designed to include students who have dual sensory impairments and/or profound learning difficulties, and provides a planning framework for organising sensory information, and for organising groups based on the needs and levels of functioning of individual students.

Individuals with profound learning difficulties are usually functioning at a pre-language and pre-symbolic level of development, and may not be communicating intentionally. They are heavily reliant on others to interpret their needs and interests. The onus is therefore on you as storyteller to create meanings for the student at whatever level is appropriate.

Students with these difficulties are likely to find the following strategies helpful:

- Smell cues. These have to be planned carefully because some smells linger on, and too many smells are confusing. You could use one smell, such as mint, to signify the beginning and the ending of a session, and one other smell to convey a particular atmosphere – for example, coconut oil for a desert island, burnt porridge for the opening scene of *Oliver Twist*. Be careful about food smells if you are not planning to give people the same food to eat, as this may a) raise hopes b) confuse with everyday events such as coffee time or dinner.

- Tactile cues. Make sure that there are some concrete representations to illustrate a story, character or poem, such as contrasting fabrics, or objects to handle. Chris Fuller (*Bag Books*) has developed tactile stories through the use of collections of objects linked to a simple narrative (see Appendix 3).
- Physical participation. Think about dramatising stories and poems through different kinds of touch and movement. For example, Romeo and Juliet's first meeting involves a palm to palm touch; in the Zeffirelli film they strain to touch hands from the balcony; their linked hands can be dragged apart by their respective families to dramatise their separation.
- Slow pace. Plan at first to do only one or two activities in a session, and build up gradually.

Finally, all students who have some understanding of the progress of their own lives and their relationships with other people will be helped by explicit links between their own experience, or contemporary news stories, and events and feelings in literature.

There are teachers, therapists and learning support assistants all over the country who are experimenting with literature. Mostly, of course, people are too busy to put their ideas in writing, which is a shame, because we can all benefit from each other's creativity and ideas. The following accounts have been put together as illustrations of approaches which have proved successful with a range of students. They prove that once you get really interested, almost any text you can think of has something to offer.

Gulliver's Travels

Carolyn Fyfe, speech and language therapist at Queen Elizabeth II Jubilee School, developed a series of 'themed groups' on the topic of adventures in literature, called *New Horizons* (Fyfe 1996). The resource includes ideas for working with *The Hobbit, The Odyssey* and *Gulliver's Travels*. *Gulliver's Travels* was used with a group who needed work on social skills.

Journey to Lilliput

Emphasise the size difference between Gulliver and the little people of the island. Demonstrate by showing a doll's house sized bed and asking the group to guess how many of these put together he would have needed; show a play person's cup, fill it with water, and ask if this would quench their thirst. Show a handkerchief and say that this is one of the Lilliputian's sheets – how many would it take to make a sheet big enough for Gulliver? Then ask the group to 'shrink', and take a large blanket or sheet and throw it over the group. This is what Gulliver's handkerchief would have been like to the little people.

Present the factionalism between the Blefuscans and the Lilliputians in this way: find out from the group something which divides them. In our group, we found out that one person liked Michael Jackson, and another hated him, but liked Boyzone. The group then naturally split itself into two groups supporting the different singers, with the two therapists also splitting off. The leaders of the groups then encouraged the two factions to argue about the issue and make sweeping generalisations (e.g. all those who like Michael Jackson are boring, silly people who should be locked up). The group with the King is the more powerful one, and he can put the others in prison (a ring of chairs) and force them to wear badges to single them out. Afterwards, the group must resolve the dispute, but without resorting to violence. Is it fair that these people should be treated like that, because they like different music?

A Christmas Carol

Rosie Brown from Kingsbury School developed a series of lessons, using some of her own ideas, and those of Park (1998) with a group of students with moderate, severe and profound learning difficulties.

Scrooge and Bob Cratchit

Bob Cratchit asks Scrooge for the day off on Christmas Day, and wishes him a Merry Christmas.

Theme: Unwillingness to share; contrast between meanness and generosity.

Activities: In pairs, pupils take on the roles of Bob Cratchit and Scrooge. Bob asks for money, Scrooge refuses and sends him away. Bob says 'Merry Christmas', and Scrooge says 'Bah! Humbug!' (use a simple communication aid for pupils with no speech). After a time, pupils reverse roles.

Pupils with profound learning difficulties: adults offer something, then snatch it away, saying 'Bah! Humbug!'

Skills: working in pairs, role play different feelings and behaviour, asking for things.

Resources: Black cloak for Scrooge, tinsel for Bob, money bags. Dim the lights and use gloomy music to create atmosphere.

Art work: Christmas decorations and display of words offered by pupils to describe Scrooge.

The Hound of the Baskervilles

Jane Grecic from Coppice SLD school used *The Hound of the Baskervilles* with a group of Key Stage 3 pupils. Sessions followed a similar format each week, usually starting in the classroom, recapping on the story so far, doing short pieces of drama in small groups, or completing worksheets. Pupils with profound and multiple learning difficulties were provided with sensory activities such as massage to music using props from 'the moor', or following sensory trails as clues.

The group then moved to a darkened room which they entered by crossing the 'grimpen mire' (green paper towels representing the safe grassy path across the moor). Pupils shouted encouragement and assisted their peers across.

Then the story was told, using sensory props, and always lit only by candlelight. Each week the atmosphere was slowly built up by listening to wind sounds, putting on hats and scarves to keep warm, and feeling the soil and leaves.

The language used for the story was a mixture of a simplified version, passages of original text from an audiotape version, and pupils' own retelling.

Some interactive games were used as well, including:

Grandmother's Footsteps – the pupil at the front being the hound with a piece of fur fabric; others had to sneak up without being heard.

Hide and seek – the 'Hound' hid in the dark, wearing the fur, while others took it in turns to try and locate him or her by listening to where the howling was coming from (the sound was programmed onto a Big Mac switch where necessary).

Looking for clues

The concepts of detectives and clues were explained, and then the pupils were offered a reward (a sweet) for having worked so hard. However, when she came to look, the teacher discovered that the sweets were missing from her bag. Pupils then followed a trail of clues (written, pictorial and sensory) to hunt for the missing sweets.

Worksheets

Simple worksheets were a mixture of pictures to colour, opportunities for free drawing, and copy writing. These were made into individual books for pupils.

Resources

Candle lantern; sound effects tapes for wind noises, wolf howls; electric fan; bowl of potting compost; leaves, twigs; green paper towels for the path across the moor; black fur fabric for the Hound; long bristly brush (its paw); 'Dragon's breath' bottled smell for its breath (any disgusting smell will do); hats and scarves for costumes.

Teacher's comments

I am still amazed at the amount of information about the story that pupils have remembered: the 'big bad dog' has become a bit of a joke in school as I was, and still am, literally 'hounded' by pupils asking for it again. I feel the success of the book lay in the fact that it was a thriller – each week, pupils were taken to the point of total terror and back again in complete safety (similar to riding the big dipper). The anticipation of the session for many pupils started with them asking/signing to me about it as they got off the transport on a Monday morning, and this continued throughout the week until the session on a Friday morning (it even helped some of our pupils learn the days of the week!).

Kubla Khan

At Moor House school, Sally Blackah, Joanna Sebire and Sue Brady worked on Coleridge's *Kubla Khan* for a term with a class of 14–15 year old students with specific language impairments. They chose the poem because of its visual nature and fantastical imagery.

The pleasure dome

The poem was read aloud several times in its entirety, to contextualise the quotations within the narrative. The style of delivery was intentionally dramatic, to help the students access the atmosphere of the poem. The students were divided into two groups to work on displays, one on 'paradise' and one on 'hell'. They used images from the text and their own conceptual realisations to create a three-dimensional display. To evoke an emotional response to the work, 'dark' and 'light' music was played to the respective groups. The final product was this visual display. Working on the poem involved using a mixture of sensory inputs – visual, auditory and tactile. It served as a meaningful introduction to pre-20th century literature.

Activities to accompany the project included:

Opposites: classification of enlarged quotations from the text into positive and negative categories:

Positive	Negative
'fertile land'	'close your eyes with holy dread'
'deep delight'	'turmoil'
'blossomed many an incense bearing tree'	'ancestral voices prophesying war'

This activity led to much discussion about opposites and extremes. Certain quotations were much more difficult to classify because of the conflicting imagery, for example 'a sunny pleasure dome with caves of ice'. This led to further discussion about differences of opinion, and the recognition that certain things cannot be easily categorised.

Drawing. Students drew the dome and its surrounding areas to represent positive aspects (inner calm) and negative aspects (outer calm). This allowed the students to individually interpret the written image visually.

Poetry workshop

A poetry workshop was held for younger pupils at Kingsbury SLD school, using: Kit Wright's *Red Boots on*, H. H. Munro's *Overheard on a Salt Marsh*, and the traditional Scottish poem *The Strange Guest*.

Red Boots on was adapted by using placenames around Wigan, where the children lived, and by including each child in the group in turn, using the colour of their footwear. The rest of the group clapped the rhythm of the poem:

Red Boots on: Original text	*Red Boots on:* Adapted text
Way down Geneva	Way down Kingsbury
All along Vine	Along Tontine
Deeper than the snowdrift	Deeper than the snowdrift
Love's eyes shine	Love's eyes shine
Mary Lou's walking	Kevin is walking
In the wintertime	In the wintertime
She's got	He's got
Red boots on	Black shoes on
She's got	He's got
Red boots on	Black shoes on
Kicking up the winter,	Kicking up the winter,
till the winter's gone.	till the winter's gone.

For Overheard on a Saltmarsh, we used some real 'green glass beads' on a necklace, which was held out for pupils to reach towards and touch. The group joined in with the refrains 'Give me' and 'No', using speech, sign and communication aids. (The one pupil who did not seem to be enjoying the experience temporarily took on the role of the goblin lying howling in the reeds.)

Overheard on a Saltmarsh by Herbert Reed
Nymph, Nymph, what are your beads?
Green glass, goblin. Why do you stare at them?
Give them me.
           No.
Give them me. Give them me.
               No...

For *The Strange Guest* a particularly talented member of staff drew the parts of
the appearing troll as they were named in the poem (see Figure 5.4) while pupils
pointed to their own body parts in chorus.

A wife was sitting at her reel one night.
And still she sat, and still she reeled, and still she wished for company.
In came a pair of big, big feet, and sat down at the fireside;
And still she sat, and still she reeled, and still she wished for company.
In came a pair of small, small knees, and sat down on the big, big feet.
And still she sat, and still she reeled, and still she wished for company...

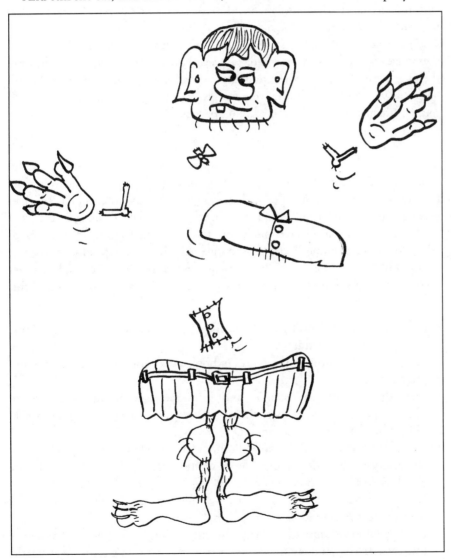

Figure 5.4 The strange guest. Original drawing by Ghislaine Grove

Wind Ted Hughes

Jane Grecic at Coppice School studied poems about the wind, focusing on the Ted Hughes poem. They experimented listening to different voices – Jane's voice, and taped voices of male relatives of staff members. The class worked through the poem each week, first exploring sound effects, then visual images (a huge art session), and finally as drama – miming activities such as walking in the wind. The poem lent itself beautifully to sound effects and imagery; pupils were given a whole range of instruments as well as common or garden objects to create sounds with – such as wobbling large sheets of card. Large painted banners were made to represent the sea and the orange sky. The group discussed the setting for the poem, and then visited Jane's house, which is a cottage on top of a hill with an open fire and a coal shed. This visit proved the highlight of the project. The students fetched coal from the shed, lit the fire, made toast and listened to the poem in the dark with only the light of the flames. They then went out into the garden and watched the wind blowing the smoke out of the chimney, as illustrated in the accompanying photographs (Figure 5.5). The sensory aspects of the visit were recalled in school using firelighters, coal and kindling to help with recall.

Other physical activities included kite flying, wind walks, using electric fans and making paper fans, windmills and model magpies hung from elastic fixed to sticks which could then be flung as described in the poem.

The students completed simple worksheets with drawings and writings of themselves flying kites in the wind. However, one student insisted on drawing the poet himself, faithfully reproducing Jane's description of him as 'wild and hairy' (Figure 5.6). Finally the students presented the poem in assembly, with some of them reading or accompanying particular lines (Figure 5.7).

Illustrating texts

There are now far more illustrated versions of classics than once was the case, for students whose vision is reasonable and who have the intellectual ability to grasp complex visual details, but it remains extremely hard to find pictures that are large enough and clear enough for students with learning difficulties to relate to the text. Some books for younger children are reproduced as large board books ('Big Books') which are suitable for showing to groups, but as yet there is nothing similar for older pupils and adults. There are ways around this problem. You can:

- enlist the help of a local school or college, to ask students to provide some large pictures to illustrate your text.
- draw round the outlines of pictures in books on overhead transparencies and project them.
- dress the students in costume and form tableaux of particular scenes. Photograph these, and project them as colour slides, or use a digital camera to capture the image on computer.
- make felt-boards with simple outlines of characters and places. The characters can be moved around as they inter-relate in different ways. Figure 5.8 shows a felt board created for *Lord Randal*, a border ballad.
- create personal books for the students using any combination of the above with the text in simple words, or symbol form.
- create your own animations with drawings, simple puppets or animation software. If the students have invested time and thought in creating the illustration, it may be more meaningful than a commercial production.

At noon I scaled along the house side as far as
The coal-house door. Once I looked up –
Through the brunt wind that dented the balls of my eyes

We watch the fire blazing
And feel the roots of the house move, but sit on
Seeing the window tremble to come in
Hearing the stones cry out under the horizons

We ended by making toast

Figure 5.5

Figure 5.6 *This is Ted Hughes – by Bryn Mulligan*

WIND – Ted Hughes
Bryn

This house has been far out at sea all night
Jessica & Kevin – sea picture

The woods crashing through the darkness, the booming hills
Sam – cymbal Laura – drum

Winds stampeding the fields under the window

Floundering black astride and blinding wet
Bryn – water spray spraying audience

Till day rose: then under an orange sky
Jessica/Kevin – sky picture

The hills had new places, and wind wielded

Blade-light, luminous black and emerald,
Ian – moves around waving ribbon

Flexing like the lens of a mad eye.

At noon I scaled along the house-side as far as
Sam with coal skuttle

The coal house door. Once I looked up
Sam miming

Through the brunt wind that dented the balls of my eyes
Still Sam

The tent of hills drummed and strained its guyrope.
Laura/Bryn drumming

The fields quivering, the skyline a grimace,

At any second to bang and vanish with a flap
– tambourine

The wind flung a magpie away and a black
Victoria/Daniel – magpies

Back gull bent like an iron bar slowly. The house

Rang like some fine green goblet in the note
Victoria – triangle

That at any second would shatter it. Now deep

In chairs in front of the great fire, we grip
—

Our hearts and cannot entertain book, thought

Or each other. We watch the fire blazing,
Turn torches on

And feel the roots of the house move, but sit on

Seeing the window tremble to come in,
Daniel with card to shake

Hearing the stones cry out under the horizons
– rainmaker

Figure 5.7

47

Figure 5.8 *Lord Randal*
Original drawing by Ghislane Grove   Photography by Mike Coles

LORD RANDAL (a Scottish traditional ballad
Oh where have you been, Lord Randal, my son?
Oh where have you been, my bonny young one?
Oh I've been to the greenwood, mother, make my bed soon
For I'm weary with hunting and I fain would lie down.

And who did you meet there, Lord Randal my son?
And who did you meet there, my bonny young one?
Oh I met with my sweetheart, mother make my bed soon
For I'm weary with hunting and I fain would lie down.

What had you for your supper, Lord Randal my son?
What had you for your supper, my bonny young one?
Eels in eel broth, mother make my bed soon
For I'm weary with hunting and I fain would lie down.

What happened to your bloodhounds, Lord Randal my son?
What happened to your bloodhounds, my bonny young one?
They stretched out their legs and died, mother make my bed soon
For I'm weary with hunting and I fain would lie down.

Oh I fear you are poisoned, Lord Randal my son.
I fear you are poisoned, my bonny young one.
Oh yes, I am poisoned, mother make my bed soon
For I'm sick to my heart and I fain would lie down.

What will you leave your mother, Lord Randal my son?
What will you leave your mother, my bonny young one?
My house and my lands, mother make my bed soon
For I'm sick to my heart and I fain would lie down.

What will you leave your sweetheart, Lord Randal my son?
What will you leave your sweetheart, my bonny young one?
Yon tow and yon halter, mother, that hangs on yon tree.
And there let her hang, for the killing of me.

There are now many good film versions available of novels and plays which you can use with pupils. However, it is important to be selective, and to take the time to explore the versions which will be most accessible to your students. For example, Jane Grecic found that the old black and white film of *Hound of the Baskervilles* was enjoyed more than a recent version in colour, because the story was told more simply and obviously. As suggested in the previous chapter, cartoon versions are often thought to be easy to follow, but in fact may prove difficult because emotions and interactions between characters are not so clearly visible, and a lot of inference may be required to bridge from one frame to another.

It is important not to make any assumptions about the ability of students to understand material presented on film, and to use the medium as a teaching tool, with discrimination. With some groups you might choose to watch the whole film (perhaps divided into parts to correspond to lessons) and then go back and revisit extracts as you work through the text in lessons. With other groups you might use the 'layering' technique (see above, p. 31), starting with a particular scene. In this case, you might tell the relevant part of the story to the group, then alert students to particular features to look for in the film, then show the scene, then review it to see what students have remembered. Once the students are familiar with the film, you can use the pause button to freeze the film and ask students what is happening, and what will happen next (if you do this the first time the film is shown it is very distracting, and students never get a feel for the whole story).

Audiotapes also offer a powerful means of transmitting novels and poetry. Again, you can choose extracts to play to students, either as a pure listening exercise, or as part of a more active presentation, perhaps by encouraging particular actions to accompany the text.

CD Roms are now available for some works of literature (see Appendix 3), and allow individuals or small groups to select and replay visual and auditory images.

Using video and audiotape

Teachers have devised many imaginative ways of encouraging their students to engage with texts (Merrick and Brennan 1993; Wade and Oates 1993). The following list is selected from some of the resources mentioned in Appendix 3.

Practical activities linked to texts

Story maps

The main events of the narrative are summarised on the wall, perhaps with large arrows or coloured ribbon to show the links (see Figure 5.9). A marker can be placed over the point in the story with which today's lesson is concerned. Students can predict some alternative developments, which can be shown as a 'crossroad' with a question mark over it.

Story boarding

Story boards are used when building up film sequences. Each main event is depicted on a separate sheet or board. This can encourage students to summarise the main events, and think about what they would include if they were filming the story. Once a story board has been created, you can actually film it, or get the students to form a tableau for a photograph.

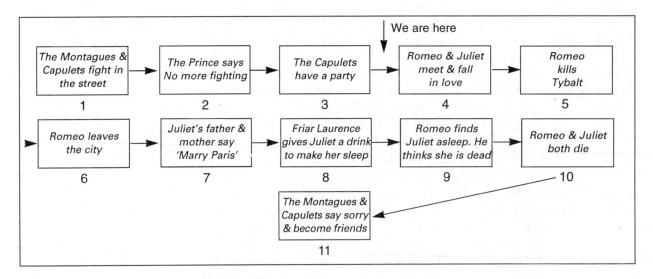

Figure 5.9 *Storyline for* Romeo and Juliet

Hot-seating

Here the action is paused, and characters are invited to take a chair and be questioned about their views of what is going on in the story.

News reports

Again, the action is paused, and students take it in turns to report on the events in the story, using a roving microphone. Reports and drawings can be presented in the form of a newspaper.

Character maps

Individual characters are created, through drawing, collage, silhouettes, photographs or any other medium suitable, and put on a display. Coloured streamers or ribbons are used to link up the characters to show their relationships – e.g. the Montagues in one circle, the Capulets in another (see Figure 5.10).

Board games

Create a board game to show the events in the story, and what happens to the characters. Players can take on the role of characters, whose counters move up and down the board depending on their fortunes. This is particularly good for adventure stories and journeys, such as *The Hobbit*, or *Pilgrim's Progress*.

Character inventions

Use what you know of a character to invent information – such as imaginary dialogues, attributes, possessions. These might be: what they would eat for dinner, the contents of a handbag, what they would say if you met them. Be careful not to be *too* anachronistic, (e.g. 'What football team does Tybalt support?') as this could be confusing for some pupils.

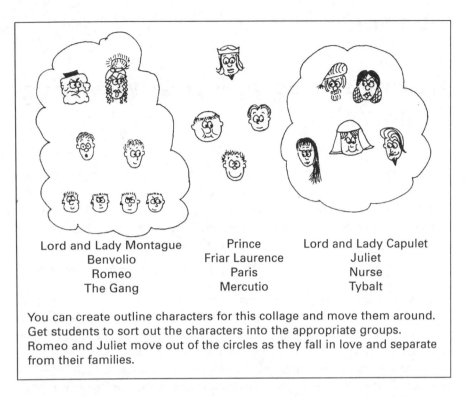

Lord and Lady Montague   Prince   Lord and Lady Capulet
Benvolio   Friar Laurence   Juliet
Romeo   Paris   Nurse
The Gang   Mercutio   Tybalt

You can create outline characters for this collage and move them around.
Get students to sort out the characters into the appropriate groups.
Romeo and Juliet move out of the circles as they fall in love and separate
from their families.

Figure 5.10 *Character map for* Romeo and Juliet, Artwork by Ghislaine Grove

Summary

This chapter has presented some practical examples of classroom projects with different groups of students with special educational needs. In the next chapter, we look at the ways of developing students' ability to produce creative writing as a response to these experiences.

CHAPTER 6

Getting started with creative writing

Tina Detheridge and Nicola Grove

> The stories of our days and the stories in our days are joined in that autobiography we are all engaged in making and remaking, as long as we live, which we never complete, though we all know how it is going to end.
> **Barbara Hardy** *Tellers and Listeners*

This chapter considers ways of supporting students in the production of creative output. This is the point at which the 'readers' of a text become the makers of new texts, through an integration of their own experiences and their imaginative engagement with a work of literature. By 'readers', of course, we mean the audience of viewers and listeners who have taken part in the activities described in the previous chapter, and demonstrated their involvement through the quality of their responses. With the right kind of support or 'scaffolding', even students with severe disabilities may be able to move beyond this level of response to creative output. In principle, such output can be expressed through many different media, such as artwork, dance, music or play making. However, there is a particular value to students in the process of writing which shapes the dynamics of language into permanent material form, and the focus in this chapter will be on types of graphic output. We have already seen some examples in the previous chapter of simple writing and drawing in response to literature. What is the value of writing – and how may skills be extended?

The power of writing

The process of writing has many functions. As well as providing a means of expression, there are some more fundamental processes which it supports. Writing is one of the mechanisms we have to store ideas; it also allows us to 'see' ideas, to sort and structure thoughts. When I go shopping I write a list. The process of constructing the list helps to fix it in my mind, so that when I get to the shop, having forgotten the list, I am able to retrieve much of the information. Similarly, if I listen to a lecture, particularly one which is quite difficult to understand, I write a lot of notes. I never read these notes. It is the act of translating someone else's ideas, selecting and structuring the key points, which helps me to understand and internalise the new concepts, as Fitzpatrick (1988) points out:

> Such expression...is creative in the usual sense of the word in that by the exercise of the imagination, something new is brought into being. In the creation of these imaginative works, children are attempting to draw on the resources of a particular medium to give heightened expression to something already clear and complete: creative activities of this kind are often a means whereby we discover what our thoughts and feelings actually are.

Writing stories or poetry is about structuring and manipulating experiences and emotions. Young children create fantasies and stories in their play, talking with their dolls or playthings, imbuing them with reality. With the formality of education, and a gradual distinction being made between 'truth' and 'fantasy', many children gradually become inhibited in such self expression. Writing stories requires the author to be able to handle the linguistics, to be able to physically form letters, and to spell and understand syntax. Stories may be more closely examined as exercises in language use and for skills shown in grammar and spelling, than for their expressive qualities. By the time they reach adolescence, many children may find writing creatively a difficult and painful experience. However, if they can be encouraged to produce their thoughts and feelings in written form, they have a means of reflecting on experience which can develop a sense of self, advance language skills, and facilitate participation in a culturally valued activity, as the story of Mabel demonstrates:

Mabel
Mabel is a chatty person, with plenty of ideas, but her sole communication is oral. She has a tendency to repeat herself, to give weight to an idea. However, she is not able to read or write text. At the Mencap and Gateway Conference, 1997, she used an overlay keyboard attached to a computer to select symbols. She could relate to these illustrations, and with very little encouragement, was able to choose and sequence them to create her own piece of writing. She listened to the text being spoken back by the computer, confirming her writing. When she was satisfied, her work was printed. It was a pity there was not a video camera on hand to capture her tremendous pleasure in holding this piece of writing which gave permanent evidence of her ideas. She read the writing back by using the symbols as reminders of what she had said, which gave her the idea that she could read other things. She immediately marched across the hall to an author displaying his work, complaining that he had not put the symbols into his book for her to read!

Being a writer, a creator of literature, confers a status on an individual. To be able to write, express your own ideas, is a dignifying process. Many children will take their stories home and parents and children get pleasure from seeing the achievement. Young people who have had little opportunity to write; who may be currently unable to physically write, recognise or spell words, or handle syntax; or who simply find the whole bundle of processes too complex, will all be excluded from the world of writers and the satisfaction that this confers, unless they can have access to alternative forms.

The main alternatives to independent writing using traditional orthography are dictation, use of symbols and pictures, and use of technology.

Forms of writing

Dictation

Ryan has moderate learning difficulties, and attends a mainstream school. His story is about a lion who lost his mane, and is full of imagination. He struggled at reading and writing, and it was beyond his current skills to be able to write an extended piece of work. Working with his support worker, he told this story. She did most of the typing to his dictation. This enabled Ryan to get the flow of his ideas, and demonstrate his creativity. Having the symbols present meant he could identify the meaning of the words he couldn't read. He then illustrated the story and it was put together into a book. This made his work look professional, conferred additional status and showed that it was valued, which in turn increased his self-esteem and confidence. Having done one story, Ryan was enthusiastic about writing rather than it being a formidable task. (See Figure 6.1.)

Figure 6.1 *Ryan's story (reprinted from Detheridge and Detheridge 1997)*

Writing through dictation, where one person expresses the ideas, and another puts them down on paper, is known technically as the use of an amanuensis, and is an important stage in building confidence in writing. It is sometimes seen as an invalid means of expression since it requires the intervention of a helper. This is, however, an unacceptable argument. Many great works of literature and music have been created in this way. It is acceptable by examining boards for pupils with severe writing problems. As time goes on more ways will become available to make the process of writing autonomous. Speech recognition systems provided by computers is one method that will give greater scope to some people who have clear and reproducible speech, but there will always be others who need help to record their creative thoughts.

Dictation can be used with either traditional orthography, symbols, drawings, or a mixture of all three.

Fiona Grey used the anthology *Caribbean Dozen*, edited by John Agard, as the inspiration for writing poetry with pupils with severe learning difficulties at St. Ann's school in Merton. First the children studied the poems, looking at the language, and using artwork to illustrate them. They then dictated their own poems, either in speech, sign or both modalities. In the re-drafting process, the poems were read back to the children, to see if they wanted to change anything, and were then submitted to the Merton Young Poets competition. Pupils attended the presentation at the town hall, and received certificates which were framed and displayed in school. The poems have been published in the anthology *Hear My Voice*. The sense of accomplishment for the students is reflected in the reaction of one boy, who was asked about himself by his new teacher, and was able to say that he had had a poem published. Figure 6.2 illustrates some of the poetry – it is notable that Stacie and Isaac dictated their poems completely in sign. Fiona feels that it was very important to build up the children's perceptions that they were going to write poems, and that their language was going to be valued as much as the words on the printed page.

A HOUSE

I can see
flowers.

I can see
flowers.

I can see
flowers.

I can see
a tree.

I can see
flowers.

I can see
a house.

I can see
paper.

I can see
a window.

I can see
flowers.

I can see
flowers.

Stacie.

A HOUSE

Flowers, rain, trees
Window, window, window,
Door
A house.

Charles.

DAD GOES TO THE SHOPS

A house
and
Two chocolate ice-cream trees.

Dad is going on the train
Dad is going to the shops
To buy a cake.

He-Man is fighting.

The key opens the door
Isaac and Mum have dinner.

Mum goes to bed.

Isaac.

HOUSE NUMBER 12

At house number 12
There are 2 trees.
Number 2 is on the door.

At house number 12
There is sand on the ground
And blue sky.

At house number 12
There are 2 plants.
It's a hot day.

Ben.

Figure 6.2 *Merton young poets from St. Ann's School*

Using symbols

Pictures and graphic symbols provide ways of expressing ideas in written, retrievable form for pupils who cannot read or write using traditional orthography. These techniques are liberating as there are currently no (formal) syntactical or grammatical rules. A student trying to explain in symbols that it was 'very windy' did so by repeating the symbol for windy, i.e. 'windy windy'. This is very expressive, but not grammatical in a formal sense. Carpenter (1997), shows how symbols functioned to provide a bridge to literacy, in a description of his daughter Katie's production of a book about her own family:

> The engagement in the reading process, we are sure, contributed to the development of her spoken language. The symbols gave Katie a perceptual bridge; an opportunity to progress in the literacy curriculum. She was not capable of the intellectual leap, demanded by conventional reading approaches, of going from picture to word... Visual languages, such as signing and symbols are the most powerful modes of development of literacy that we can offer them (Carpenter 1997).

The use of pictures or symbols as cues can facilitate participation in other literacy activities. Shirley Austin has written plays to support the learning of her pupils. The Roman Play they wanted to perform is quite long. The pupils would find it hard to learn their parts without a great deal of help. Having the text with symbol support means they can read the script. The Christmas play at another school was printed with each part in a different colour so that it was easy to identify each character. The symbols there were used as cues to the ideas. These pupils would not remember the words, but were at least cued in to the appropriate content of their next speech – ensuring that the flow of the story kept along the right lines.

Using objects

Myles Pilling has used memory objects as a basis for creating stories with pupils at Rainbow School in Kent. An object associated with a particular event is brought in for a 'show and tell' session with the group, and used as the basis for discussion: is the object old or new? what is it for? make up a drama about the object. For example, a war helmet has a dent in it – how did it get there?

Using technology

Word banks or word lists can present vocabulary as a stimulus. An on-screen grid with words and pictures can encourage greater experimentation with vocabulary. It is an easier step to be presented with words to choose from than having to conjure them up in your mind. This is particularly helpful to the less confident writer. This example uses a grid program called Point, used for a Romeo and Juliet storyline (see Figure 6.3). The teacher can simply type lists of words and

Figure 6.3 *Point grid for writing about Romeo and Juliet*

the software will automatically arrange them in the screen display ready for the student to select. Telling the story and communicating is the essential thing. Dave Wood at Wilson Stuart school is firmly of the opinion that the children need to experience story telling before they can refine the skills. In their nursery the children use an overlay keyboard with symbol writing software to produce 'scribble' or 'pretend' writing before they even learn to recognise symbols as part of their emergent literacy experience. He also encourages the teachers to model the writing process, by writing in class, using the same technologies.

A non-speaking child engaged in a story telling activity by selecting pictures from a computer screen. A number of screens were prepared each with pictures. George could select pictures using a switch, so that as the story unfolded he could choose what happened next, or in which direction the story would go. The simplest story involved an imaginary journey. The first screen had different vehicles to indicate how they were to travel, other screens had places, items, activities, or characters. The story teller – the teacher – responded to George's selections at the appropriate time and incorporated them into the narrative. Over time the stories became longer and more complex as both the narrator and the student became more familiar with the technique.

Literacy through symbols (Detheridge and Detheridge 1997) provides many examples of creative writing produced with the help of symbols and computer technology.

Having considered some different forms which written output could take, we move to exploring ways of stimulating its production, through collaboration and the use of frameworks.

Group writing

Our curriculum places an emphasis on individual learning and individual output. However, for those who are getting started on the process of writing, collaboration can build confidence and generate ideas, and group writing is a recognised strategy for encouraging pupils to get started (Ray 1996; Sedgwick 1992). At Wilson Stuart School, the communication group have one session where they engage in collaborative writing, learning to work together, and to communicate peer to peer, rather than child to adult. With some careful help they were given tools to write poems exploring sounds (see Figure 6.4a).

They also each wrote stories about their hopes and feelings (see Figure 6.4b). Some of these stories are very moving, sometimes giving staff the first glimpse of the depth of feelings these children have. Keeping a sense of humour, having jokes and their responses programmed into the communication aids helped the children join in exchanges with their peers. Life can sometimes seem rather too serious if you are not given the tools to laugh, joke and mess around

At Wilson Stuart, each child's stories are put into non-reflective plastic wallets to make them more durable. Ring binders are used, partly because it is easier to turn the pages but also it allows pages to be added. The children build up personal books about their lives and interests (see Figure 6.5).

Students can use whatever they like to communicate – photographs, cuttings, symbols. Jane Grecic, as part of the activities associated with *The Hound of the Baskervilles* at Coppice School, worked on the anonymous letter sent to Sir Henry Baskerville, which uses the time-honoured technique of cutting out individual words and letters from a newspaper. Pupils then created their own letters, or simply cut out the letters for their names.

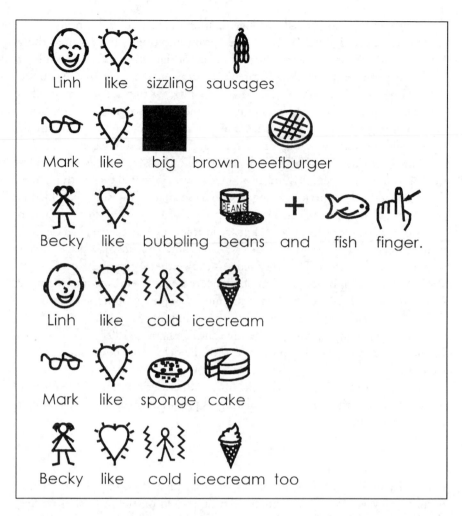

Figure 6.4(a) Wilson Stuart School communication group: exploring sounds and feelings

At Cheyne School for pupils with physical disabilities, Helen Cockerill, the speech therapist, ran a poem group each week with a group of five and six year olds. Again, the children were provided with a strong framework, using concept keyboard overlays with Bliss symbols to support choices, with grammatical colour coding. Eventually this led to more creative output, as illustrated by the poem 'Chocolate feet; sticky hands', where the lines were contributed spontaneously by the children. After the group, the computer printouts were made into books.

CHOCOLATE FEET AND STICKY HANDS
by **Jodie**, **Daniel** and **Adam**

I want cold feet.
I want sticky hands.
I want!

I don't want chocolate feet.
I don't want lots of hands.
I don't want!

You and me don't want sticky hands.
You and me don't want lots of feet.

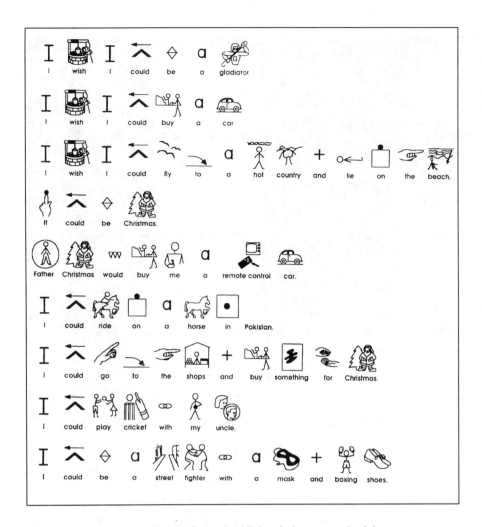

The symbols above spell out, line by line:

I wish I could be a gladiator

I wish I could buy a car

I wish I could fly to a hot country and lie on the beach.

It could be Christmas.

Father Christmas would buy me a remote control car.

I could ride on a horse in Pakistan.

I could go to the shops and buy something for Christmas.

I could play cricket with my uncle.

I could be a street fighter with a mask and boxing shoes.

Figure 6.4(b) *Wilson Stuart School: children's hopes and wishes*

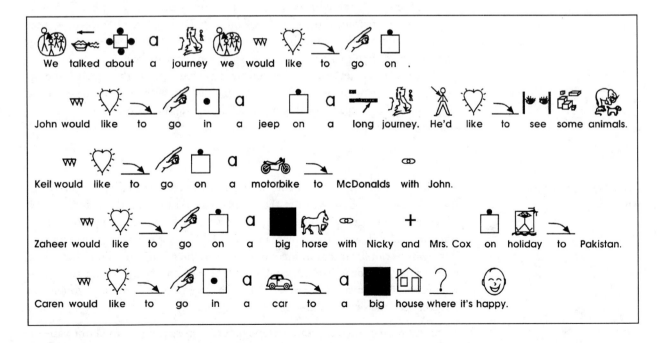

The symbols above spell out, line by line:

We talked about a journey we would like to go on .

John would like to go in a jeep on a long journey. He'd like to see some animals.

Keil would like to go on a motorbike to McDonalds with John.

Zaheer would like to go on a big horse with Nicky and Mrs. Cox on holiday to Pakistan.

Caren would like to go in a car to a big house where it's happy.

Figure 6.5 *Personal stories from Wilson Stuart School*

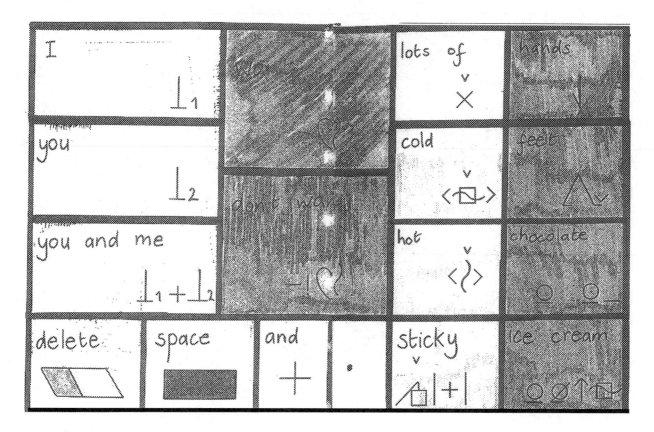

Figure 6.6 *Concept keyboard overlay for 'Chocolate Feet and Sticky Hands'*

Figure 6.6 illustrates the overlay which was used to create this poem.

Group writing with dictation was used at Heathermount School for autistic pupils, to create a poem after a workshop on *Macbeth*. There were seven boys in the group, varying in ability, and we built up the poem through fragments of what they remembered from the text, and the associated activities. Words in italics were contributed by staff (see Figure 6.7). It is worth recording that Donald, who started and finished the poem for us, is a silent boy who generally finds it very difficult to participate in groups and stay on task.

The sense of achievement conveyed by these students as they each came up to read out the poem we had created provided us with one of those magic moments which keeps you going as a teacher despite the pressures of paperwork and inspections.

Frameworks and prompts

Mention has already been made of the use of word banks and overlays as scaffolds for emergent writing. There many variations of these techniques, which essentially rely on providing progressively larger and larger slots which students can fill with their own inventions. The scripts which provide the frameworks can be programmed onto communication aids, and then onto overlays or grids for writing. King-DeBaun (1990) and Musselwhite and King-DeBaun (1997) have suggested several innovative ways of involving students in the creation of stories and poems:

- 'round robins': each student has one part of a story programmed onto an aid, and the story unfolds as each person contributes. Students can also read from symbol scripts to join in this activity.

> *How shall we start our poem?*
>
> **Donald:** Hubble, bubble, toilet trouble[1]
> *Fire burn and cauldron bubble.*
> *Night noises*
> **Anthony:** As Macbeth walks through.
> *Vampires.*
> **Donald:** Ha ha ha.
> **Anthony:** Screeching doors screech here and there.
> **Peter:** There's an owl
> *Too-whit too-whoo*
> **Anthony:** Macbeth draws closer.
> *As wolves howl.*
> **Peter:** Wind
> *Blows and whistles, whew.*
> *As Macbeth is killing sleep.*
> **Anthony:** Macbeth is king and here comes trouble.
> **Donald:** Knock on the door! Move it on the double!
>
> So the finished poem looks like this:
>
> Hubble, bubble, toil and trouble
> Fire burn and cauldron bubble.
> Night noises as Macbeth walks through.
> Vampires – ha ha ha
> Screeching doors screech here and there
> There's an owl – too-whit too-whoo
> Macbeth draws closer
> As wolves howl.
> Wind blows and whistles, whew.
> As Macbeth is killing sleep.
> Macbeth is king, and here comes trouble.
> Knock on the door! Move it on the double!
> Hubble, bubble, toil and trouble
> Fire burn and cauldron bubble.

Figure 6.7 *Macbeth poem – Heathermount School*

- story scripts and story frames: use conventional scripts to build a story outline, into which novel elements can be slotted (see Figure 6.8).
- story comments: stop the story at key points and have comments programmed onto communication aids. Musselwhite suggests that, initially, responses should be pre-selected so that all choices are correct, until students are familiar with the techniques and can interject their own ideas.

When the stories have been created orally, they can be put into written form by the students themselves or a helper. A tape recorder or video (to record signs or gestures) is an invaluable way of providing a record of the session.

Once students are familiar with a story line, and can contribute elements to it, they may be able to engage in more structured activities related to texts, such as the following, suggested by Shirley Austin from Marshlands School, who supports pupils with special educational needs in primary schools. Together, pupils and teachers make small story books on a single sheet of A4 paper which is folded into four to make pages. Each page has one or two sentences, supported with symbols as appropriate. Space is left for the pupil to illustrate the writing, to copy it or to add more. The pupils then share their stories with others in the class, giving everyone several to choose from. These may be based on pupils' personal experiences, or a book or poem. The shared text can then be used in a variety of ways as a source for learning (see Figure 6.9).

---

[1] We engaged in some discussion to resolve this understandable confusion before the final version of the poem was agreed.

1. A dark dark night

It was a dark dark night
Alice and Jarwed and Sharon were sitting at home, **when suddenly**
There was a knock on the door
Who is knocking on the door?
Alice opened the door
Nobody there!
Alice went out to look

It was a dark dark night
Jarwed and Sharon were sitting at home, **when suddenly**
There was a knock on the door
Who is knocking on the door?
Jarwed opened the door
Nobody there!
Jarwed went out to look

It was a dark dark night
Sharon was sitting at home, **when suddenly**
There was a knock on the door
Who is knocking on the door?
Sharon opened the door
Nobody there!
Sharon went out to look

It was a dark dark night
Where is Alice?
Where is Jarwed?
Where is Sharon?
Who is knocking on the door?
You say!

In this story frame, the scripts are programmed onto communication aids. The three named students perform the actions as the storyteller narrates. The final denouement is decided by the group – and might change each week.

2. Consequences
a person...went somewhere...met someone...did something...and the consequence was...

This story frame was used with a group of three students with moderate/severe learning difficulties, using their own preferences for activities and stars. For the final sequence, they dressed up in the appropriate gear and had their photographs taken. The results were made into books for them. The students had to select their alternatives from magazine pictures, and also decide which activities were appropriate for each student.

Dave	Anna	Richard
went	**went**	**went**
to Arsenal	to a disco	to a club
met	**met**	**met**
Tony Adams	Take That	James Bond
scored a goal	danced all night	played cards
and then...	**and then...**	**and then...**
won the cup	went to Bermuda	got the girl

3. I woke up one morning

I woke up one morning
I went downstairs
and I saw...
snow/ a lion/ a feast/ a flood

act out what happens next
then write about it.

This story frame was used week by week, first using only one activity until the students were familiar with it, then building on the students' own imagination.

Figure 6.8 *Some examples of story framing*

Write a story or poem in symbols.

Familiarise the children with the story – read to them – read together – children then read alone. Ask questions about the story.
When the child is familiar with the story, choose some of the activities below.

- Cloze procedure – read through and explain carefully. Child to cut and stick missing words into the correct place.
- What's wrong? Child to read the story and see where words have been put in silly places. Put a cross through wrong words.
- Give the child a copy of the story. Get him to change some words or even lines.
- Cut the story into strips for the child to sequence.
- Remove any common words the child is learning, use as a spelling exercise.
- Remove initial sounds for child to fill in.
- Make the story into a book form for the child to illustrate. Give the child one to take home.

Figure 6.9 Structured activities related to texts

A Y3 class teacher used one of Shirley's poems about the wind with her pupils, a lot of whom have learning problems. The more able children were able to suggest words for the sounds the wind makes. The poem was put into the usual story format with space for the children to add their own verse to the poem. The children enjoyed this activity and got a lot out of it at their own level. Further activities involve pasting the lines onto card, sequencing them, asking them to reason about the text, such as whether it matters in which order the lines go?

Having symbols gives support for these pupils struggling with text. As they become familiar with the words the symbols are removed, cueing them just enough to be able to complete the activity, but at the same time giving them the chance to handle vocabulary. One child in particular gained the confidence to attempt a few lines of writing in class which he had not previously done. He is still struggling to gain a sight vocabulary, but the symbol support gave him access. The aim of this approach, Shirley identifies, is:

- to build self esteem through almost instant success gained by reading with symbols;
- to develop an interest in reading and stories;
- to develop the use of context and syntax cues in reading;
- to develop phonological awareness;
- to be able to pick out the main idea from a piece of text.

Using photographs and video

Because video and television are so much a part of students' lives, they can provide a familiar and valued way of starting stories. For example, one group of secondary students with learning difficulties wrote a story based on an incident in a soap. They then acted the story, taking photographs of the key scenes. These pictures were scanned into the computer and dialogue added in speech bubbles. The resulting comic strip book was creative, interesting and well presented, giving a real feeling of self-esteem to the authors.

In the United States, Ted Hasslebring from Vanderbilt University used video as a basis for story telling and writing with a group of students with learning difficulties. Using a similar approach to Shirley Austin's, they watched a cartoon with their teachers and parents, to become familiar with the events. Stills taken from the video were then printed to give them reminders and tools for re-telling, first to re-sequence the action, using the cards as cues for telling the story. They then used the images on the computer to provide the illustrations for their own re-writing of the story. Finally they were encouraged to write a new story using some of the cards if they wanted, by changing some aspects of the original. The structured approach slowly built confidence, and let the pupils face one new challenge at a time.

The above suggestions represent only a small selection of the ideas that are available for developing emergent literacy in students with special educational needs. Many other strategies can be found in resources produced to support reading and writing in mainstream schools, a list of which is provided in Appendix 3.

Summary

This chapter has been concerned with starting points for writing. Once students become more confident, they may be able to engage in more sustained sequences of storytelling and poetry, either in written or oral form, and thus move into narrative. Knowing how to construct a narrative is a critical skill for framing our experiences in ways that can be shared with others, and the next chapter will summarise some research findings which provide a relevant framework for helping students to tell and re-tell stories.

CHAPTER 7

Looking at narratives

> I wish, my dear sister and my Lord the King, that there were more time to tell you also the story of the Fisherman and the Brass Bottle, for it is really much better and more wonderful than this tale...
>
> **Amabel Williams Ellis** *The Tale of Queen Sharazad*

Queen Sharazad saved herself from the threat of execution each dawn by engrossing her husband with tales of the Arabian Nights. White (1980) suggests that the recall of events is fashioned into a story through the introduction of a problem-solving scenario, involving a beginning, an ending and central figures. It has been suggested in the opening chapters to this book that the sharing of stories lies at the heart of our social and linguistic identity, and there is plenty of evidence to suggest that children's narratives reveal their knowledge of social and cultural experiences and conventions (Heath 1982; McCabe and Peterson 1991). For example, N., a seven year old Pushto speaker had been identified as a slow learner with language difficulties. She ended a re-telling in Pushto of Quentin Blake's *Patrick* with the sentence 'And that is the ending', which the interpreter identified as a traditional form of story conclusion (Campion 1997). Although she had significant problems in learning, N. had picked up an important skill that allowed her to take part appropriately in a valued activity. Knowing how to frame stories is important for social inclusion, and is also critical to the development of language and literacy (Snow 1983). In educational contexts, children are faced with the tasks of talking about their experiences and what they have read or seen, whether in Science, History or English. The skills involved in narrative are not only cognitive (e.g. recall and sequencing) and linguistic (e.g. the mastery of structures for connecting clauses), but specific and conventional. N. had learned how a story should be told in a particular social context.

One of our main strategies for eliciting responses to literature is to ask students to re-tell a story, or to make up their own. In the previous chapter, we looked at some ways of scaffolding participation in writing and storytelling for beginning authors. Narrative recall is prominent among the skills demanded by the English National Curriculum, featuring from Key Stage 1 to Key Stage 4, and is required at Level 1 for Speaking and Listening ('accounts') and Level 2 for Writing ('communicating meaning in both narrative and non-narrative forms') (See Figure 7.1). If we want to develop the ability of our pupils to frame their experience as stories, we need to have some idea about how storytelling develops in young children, and a system for describing and analysing narrative

Narrative skills

techniques. This chapter provides a review of relevant research findings on the emergence of narrative skills, both in typically developing children, and children with special educational needs.

Speaking and Listening
KS1
Range telling stories, both real and imagined; describing events, observations and experiences
Key skills incorporate relevant detail in explanations, descriptions and narratives, taking into account the needs of their listeners

KS2
Range telling and enacting stories and poems; reporting and describing events and observations
Key skills recall and re-present important features of an argument, talk, presentation, reading, radio or television programme

KS3/4
Range explanation, description and narration
Key skills adapt presentation to different audiences; structure talk...using a range of markers to aid the listener

Writing
KS1
Range variety of narratives e.g. stories, diaries, and records e.g. observations
Key skills organise imaginative and factual writing in different ways

KS2
Range use the characteristics of different kinds of writing, including imaginative writing and non-fiction
Key skills develop their ability to organise and structure writing, using their experience of fiction, poetry and other texts

KS3/4
Range write for aesthetic and imaginative purposes
Key skills to develop their ability to write narrative, pupils should be encouraged to draw on their experience of good fiction, develop their use of techniques, use their knowledge of story structure, description of settings, organisation of plot and means of conveying characters and relationships.

Figure 7.1 Narrative demands in the English National Curriculum

Children seem to begin telling stories very early indeed. Ruth Weir (1962) collected bedtime monologues from her two year old son. By this age, children can actually distinguish different types of narrative, or genres, in their productions. At first these have the character of 'scripts' (see p. 15), recalling what usually happens in generalised events (Nelson 1986), but between the ages of two and three they begin to recount personal events, provide on-line commentaries which narrate the events in their play, and tell fictional stories (Allen *et al.* 1994; Fox 1993; Hicks 1990). Between the ages of three and four, children's narratives become more independent of the supporting script, but are still somewhat confused and lacking in critical inferences. Control over narrative structures, conventions and pragmatic demands increases with age. By the age of ten, most children are able to tell complex stories which are structurally coherent, and which are adapted to the needs of different audiences (Reilly *et al.* 1990). Various approaches have been taken to the analysis of stories

(Applebee 1978; Berman 1988; Fox 1993; Mandler and Johnson 1977; Stein and Glenn 1979). Figure 7.2 illustrates one proposed sequence of development, adapted from Westby *et al.* (1989). What, then, are the features which differentiate between early and mature narratives?

Cognitive processes	Story telling skills
1. Ability to label.	Naming of events as single items, or brief descriptors of objects, people, places. No structural relationships between items.
2. Awareness of the distinction between animate (acts) and inanimate (acted upon).	Sequences of actions may be described, sometimes following the order in which they were perceived. A central theme or character may be discernible.
3. Some understanding of cause and effect relationships, and linear time.	'Chaining' begins: a sequence of chronological actions which are causally linked, but without any evidence of intentions or goals 'and then...and then...'
4. Awareness of psychological causality develops – i.e. that emotions give rise to actions; that certain situations cause emotions, and that actions are undertaken in pursuit of goals. Awareness of immediate future. Awareness of stock characteristics associated with scripts – e.g. heroes and villains in fairy stories. Understanding of basic emotions – anger, joy, fear, sadness.	Cause and effect relationships are evident. Story structures emerge – a problem, an initiating event, and consequences. Reference may be made to intentions of characters.
5. Insight into complex relationships between characters and context, leading to unpredictable events. Understanding of the need to provide explanations for events and behaviour. Understanding of more complex emotions – jealousy, guilt. Understanding of time frames – days, weeks etc.	Stories contain references to goals and intentions, and the internal responses of characters, as well as external events and consequences.
6. Awareness that people change as a result of what happens to them. Awareness of distinction between appearance and reality (deceit and trickery). Awareness of multiple meanings, and distinction between literal and figurative language.	Stories become more elaborate, with multiple episodes, or reflecting more than one point of view.
7. Ability to reflect on the story as a story - 'metanarrative skill'; themes, characters, differences of interpretations, and messages (eg. allegories, fables).	

Figure 7.2 Developmental sequence for story telling

Analysing storytelling – two perspectives

In an early study of adult narratives of personal experience, Labov and Weletsky (1967) suggested that there were two dimensions to skilled storytelling. The first is *referential*, concerned with the information content of the story, and the second is *affective*, concerned with the feelings the narrator has about the story. When we look at *referential structure*, we are interested in the extent to which stories are structured around goals: the inclusion of key events and characters in an appropriate setting, the ways in which the story hangs together in connected or causal sequences, the definition of a problem and its resolution. These are the features which are analysed through story 'grammars' (Mandler and Johnson 1977) and their associated linguistic devices (Berman 1988).

When we look at the *affective* dimension, we are concerned with the value of the event as a personal experience (Allen *et al.* 1994). It is emotional colour which provides us with the meaning and significance of the story, which otherwise comes over as nothing more than a bald sequence of events (Reilly *et al.* 1990), in Fox's words: '...a Gradgrindish model, rejecting those very elements to do with expression and affects which may have a profound effect on the listener and condition what is recalled' (p. 70).

The storyteller who has productive control over affective devices, is able to engage the attention of the listener, emphasising the high points of the story by introducing such features as pausing, contrastive stress and linguistic devices which indicate the attitudes and mental states of the protagonists, as well as the viewpoint of the narrator.

These two dimensions are loosely related, in that more complex narratives tend to show more sophisticated affective structures. However, in general there is only a modest relationship between them (Peterson and McCabe 1983). Stories which are very fragmentary, such as those of three year olds, may be told with high levels of affect, whereas stories with more developed event structure may come over as bland and unengaging (Reilly *et al.* 1990).

Appendix 4 provides a framework that can be used to explore levels of narrative competence in oral, signed or graphic modes of communication.

Storytelling by pupils with special needs

It is only fairly recently that an interest has been shown in narrative production by people with different types of developmental disabilities. What is apparent is that young people with special needs of varying levels of severity can produce narratives, but their ability to master the associated structural devices, whether referential or affective, will differ. Children with language delays and difficulties have problems with recalling and coordinating information (Loveland and Tunali 1993). Children with Williams' syndrome, who are characterised by precocious linguistic skills compared to their performance on nonverbal tasks, produce narratives which have rich and complex structures both in the referential and the affective domain. Children with Down's syndrome can reproduce some narrative detail, but they often seem to miss the main point, include irrelevant information, and fail to make the sequence of events into a story. They are also much less likely to enrich their stories with either prosodic or linguistic affective devices (Reilly *et. al* 1990; Fabbretti *et al.* 1997). On the other hand, once mental age has been taken into account, children with Down's syndrome seem to be quite comparable to younger children in their abilities to include details about main characters. Children with autism tend to relate stories which show connectivity, but, as would be predicted, are strikingly lacking in affect (Loveland and Tunali 1993).

However, we should be wary of making too many predictions on the basis of categories of special need, or level of ability, given that so little comparative data is available from special populations, and that relatively little attention has been paid to how narrative skills might be taught to children with more severe disabilities, whose language abilities are limited. Because affect is carried through paralinguistic features of intonation, stress, gesture and facial expression, and because features of a story can be conveyed through mime, it is in fact possible to tell an engrossing story with very little language. For example, Andreas, a man with moderate learning difficulties, no speech, and gross use of gesture, provided a vivid account of how he was mugged on a bus, using space to show where he was sitting, and how the man approached him (referential aspects) and intense and emphatic gestures, vocalisation and expressions to convey his feelings (affective aspects).

Students with learning difficulties can frequently recall isolated aspects of an event or story, but lack the skills and experience to construct a sequence. When appropriate intervention is provided, it appears that both typically developing children and those who have learning difficulties can improve their ability to tell stories ((Hemphill *et al.* 1994). Moreover, the contexts in which stories are elicited, the materials which are used, and the type of story required all have an effect on the extent to which children deploy their potential skills.

Intervention strategies: enabling narrative competence

Genre

Genre refers to the different types of stories that children are required to tell. Allen and her colleagues (1994) found that children produced more narratives with multiple episodes and action sequences in fictional than in personal event stories, where more descriptive sequences and complete episodes were included. This may be because in personal events there is more involvement of visual memory, and events are recalled as single complete wholes. Hicks (1990) compared primary school children's ability to produce an ongoing commentary for a film, a news report, and recall of a filmed narrative. The children used more affective devices in the storytelling task, and were less likely to connect events causally in the ongoing commentary.

Materials

Sequences of pictures are perhaps the commonest prompt given to children to elicit narratives. It may be, however, that this task is not as easy as the re-telling of stories seen on film, since in the former case children have to infer links between the pictures, whereas the film allows these to unfold dynamically for the children. Moore (1997) found that both typically developing children and children with Down's syndrome produced fuller references in response to moving than still pictures displayed on video. In my own research on the use of manual signs by children with learning difficulties, a dramatic video story was successful in eliciting responses even from children with very limited expressive language ability (Grove 1995). When pictures are provided as a stimulus to primary school aged children, narrative structures tend to be less advanced than when the children tell stories from their own imagination (Spinillo and Pinto 1994), and children tend to rely on the pictures and convey less in their descriptions. There is also evidence that children's story retelling from video contains more dynamic gestures encoding actions, than stories based on pictures (Meringoff *et al.* 1983). Thus each technique has its advantages and disadvantages, and a balance needs to be struck between providing support, and providing a constraint.

Role of listener

Children are likely to produce stories which are more complex and explicit if they know that the listener is not already in possession of the salient facts. If we ask children to tell us stories when we are both looking at a set of pictures, they may take our perspective into account, make assumptions about what we know, and use more elliptical language (Schneider and Dubé 1997). Moore (1997) found that five year old children, and children with Down's syndrome, produced more explicit references when it was evident that the listener could not see the video screen that the children were watching.

Contextual support

Researchers have used a variety of ways to support children's ability to produce narratives. Essentially these are fairly similar to those suggested for creative writing, but may be used in a more extempore way. They include:

- providing a model of how to do it (tell an exemplar story; watch Sesame Street News Reports);
- providing picture prompts (e.g. photos of significant events);
- providing a story book cover and pages with minimal prompts, or blanks, which invite the child to act as storyteller;
- puppet audience or stooges;
- providing scripted 'lead-ins' (e.g. *'Once upon a time . . .'; 'I was walking down the road when . . .'*);
- providing prompts (*What happened next? And then?*).

A voice for people who lack words

An alternative perspective on narrative research is provided by Booth and Booth (1996), researchers who explore the difficulty of interviewing people who have poor memories, low self-esteem and a concrete frame of reference, about their life stories. Their subject, Danny, was unable to respond to open-ended questions, and could only participate through yes–no answers and single words. They note that stories can evolve in the absence of hard information, and that silences can be telling. 'The small particulars that Danny so sparingly relates assume . . . an emblematic status' (p. 67). Danny's story reflects the spaces in his life as much as the events, and the researchers argue that sensitive interviewing can provide an opportunity for listening to voices which are currently excluded and marginalised.

Experiences and opportunities

Perhaps the most important lesson we can learn from studies of narrative is that storytelling is a skill which emerges from experience in particular cultural contexts. Children are socialised into storytelling, by what they hear and see. Students with special needs can be helped to develop their narrative skills by the provision of appropriate prompts and contextual support, but what is vital is to provide a culture of expectation, by offering students continual opportunities for recalling and reconstructing events. Everyday events such as outings, playground incidents, surprises and accidents need to be seized on and retold, perhaps at the end of the day with a wall chart or symbol timetable. The stories of our days link to the stories of the days of our friends and families, and the days we encounter through imagination.

Research findings suggest that the ability to engage in storytelling emerges in a predictable sequence, which can be used as a basis for analysis. Such findings enable us to build on the kind of creative insights and practice which were outlined in the previous chapter, to develop systematic frameworks for evaluating the making of stories. However, the starting point for this book is the need to develop a response to literature in all learners – not only those who have the skill to relate their experiences. Evaluation is the subject of the following chapter, which seeks to develop a coherent model for conceptualising responses which is truly inclusive.

Summary

CHAPTER 8

Response to literature: a framework for evaluation

'But there is something – not an Ology at all – that your father has missed, or forgotten, Louisa. I don't know what it is. I have often sat with Sissy near me and thought about it. I shall never get its name now. But your father may...'

'Where are the graces of my soul? where are the sentiments of my heart? what have you done, O father, what have you done, with the garden that should have bloomed once, in this great wilderness here?'

Charles Dickens *Hard Times*

The purpose of assessment

Within the National Curriculum, considerable emphasis is placed on assessment of pupil responses, using hierarchical 'level descriptors' which are criterion-referenced (see Figure 8.1 for examples).

Level 1
Pupils recognise familiar words in simple texts. They use their knowledge of letters and sound-symbol relationships in order to read words and to establish meaning when reading aloud. In these activities they sometimes require support. They express their response to poems, stories and non-fiction by identifying aspects they like.

Level 2
Pupils' reading of simple texts shows understanding and is generally accurate. They express opinions about major events or ideas in stories, poems and non-fiction. They use more than one strategy, such as phonic, graphic, syntactic and contextual, in reading unfamiliar words and establishing meaning.

Level 3
Pupils read a range of texts fluently and accurately. They read independently, using strategies appropriately to establish meaning. In responding to fiction and non-fiction they show understanding of the main points and express preferences. They use their knowledge of the alphabet to locate books and find information.

Figure 8.1 *Examples of level descriptors for Reading in the English National Curriculum*

This final chapter will discuss the role of evaluation in the context of an arts-based approach to the teaching of literature, and will present a framework which allows teachers to consider the quality of a pupil's response from different perspectives.

This framework is not referenced to Key Stages and levels of attainment. This is because we really have no evidence as yet about levels of development in 'affective intelligence' (Goleman 1996) or 'intelligent sensing' (Ross 1978). Most of the work which has been done on Key Stage assessment in English, or text comprehension in the National Literacy Strategy, relates to achievements in written language, located within the cognitive domain. The levels of attainment set out in the curriculum documentation make some minimal reference to feeling states in the use of terms such as 'lively', 'imaginative', 'confident', but they are scattered randomly across levels, and there appears to be no logic in the gradations from one level to another (for example, why is pupils' writing 'lively and thoughtful' at Level 4, but only becomes 'varied and interesting' at Level 5?). Rather than attempting to grade responses to literature, the approach outlined here relies on detailed description of how pupils communicate their reactions to an experience.

There seems to be a general feeling among educators at present that so much energy is expended on assessment that there is little left for doing the actual teaching. At a workshop held to explore creative approaches to literature across the spectrum of special educational needs, the introduction of a session on assessment led to a palpable sinking of the spirits among participants; a sense that the responses that we wanted to elicit from our students would be killed stone dead by attempts to weigh and measure. The laments by Louisa Gradgrind and her mother, quoted above, are illustrative of the romantic view of what may be lost in an obsession with intellectual achievement. This unease is articulated by Swanwick (1997) in relation to the curriculum for music:

> Many people may have fears of getting caught up in the machinery of assessment and worry that the magic of music and the uniqueness to individual pupils will be compromised by being processed through the clanking apparatus of marks and grades... (p. 205).

Part of the reluctance to become embroiled in the assessment process may stem from a lack of clarity about its purpose within an arts curriculum. Assessment may be undertaken for a variety of reasons, the major categories being:

- diagnostic – to identify learning strengths and weaknesses;
- summative – to provide an absolute indication of a level of achievement;
- comparative – to compare one pupil with another, in order to ascertain levels of achievement;
- formative – to assist the process of teaching;
- evaluative – to monitor the effectiveness of teaching.

There are clearly areas of overlap between each of these categories. In the context of response to literature, the purposes of assessment are essentially *formative* and *evaluative*, for both pupil and teacher (Aspin 1981). Assessment will contribute to the process of profiling the achievements of pupils, by illustrating the contexts and the forms through which they can respond in ways that are discriminating, creative and affective. Assessment allows teachers to monitor and evaluate their work, and to see what the experience means to the people they are teaching. Are we communicating what we thought we were communicating? Is the approach working? Does it stimulate their abilities to think and feel and express themselves? Essentially, we are interested to know the effects on our students of the texts we use and the way we present them. As

Swanwick goes on to say, this is 'part of the fabric of teaching': '...all teaching involves responding appropriately to what students do and say. And responding appropriately suggests that we can in a sense "read" what is happening.' (p. 205).

'Reading what is happening' is a nice phrase for our purposes. It suggests an ongoing, dynamic, descriptive process in which we are continually trying out an approach, observing its effects and adapting what we do. From this point on, the term *evaluation* is preferred to *assessment* because it suggests an orientation to the process rather than the product. The first step is to clarify why we want to evaluate, and the type of evaluation which is appropriate. We have established that the purpose of our evaluation is to inform our own teaching, and to contribute to our knowledge of the potential of our students. This suggests that the type of evaluation which will be most useful is one which is richly descriptive of the student's response, rather than a test which the student must pass or fail. The next step is to decide what we want to know. This will depend to a large extent on what we think we are teaching, which brings us back to the conceptual framework which we are using to organise and present the experience. To recap, the approach represented in this book is based on the following principles:

• A concern with the development of aesthetic responses grounded in feeling and sensation, through which distinct ideas and reflective cognition may evolve.
• A view of literature as an experience which is social and cultural, as well as private and individualised. Students' participation and understanding grows through repeated exposure to conventional forms in contexts which support their learning.
• A view of meaning as a product of the creative interaction between the student and the text, rather than inherent in the text and accessible only to those who can crack the code. This does not imply that any and all interpretations of a text will be valid, but allows us to look at what interactions and meanings are possible for particular groups of students, and to acknowledge that everyone's experience of a text is likely to differ. What interests us is the relationship between the writer's product, the response of the individual, and the impact this has on a cultural community.

What we want to know, therefore, is how students respond to the experiences we offer them. We will be observing and evaluating all the ways in which students show reactions; not only in written output or oral narratives, but in their body language, the way they use their voices, their gestures and their facial expressions; paintings, drawings, movement, dance and song. When asked how they evaluate pupils' reactions, teachers of students with special needs invariably mention these behaviours. These are the signals which combine to provide us with information about the student's expressive response to literature.

The expressive response

Ross (1978, p. 35) defines the expressive response as 'that which represents or symbolises feeling', and considers it as the basis of the arts curriculum. The process of representation transforms *sensation* into *perceptions* or 'intelligent feeling' as outlined in Chapter 2 of this book and presented in Figure 8.2. That is, the starting point is a *sensation*, which gives rise to *feeling*, which maybe transformed into an image (visual, auditory, tactile, smell or taste) which the mind works on and considers – Do I like it? What does it remind me of? Is it the same as or different from another experience? Is it a surprise? What was just a sensation becomes a *perceptive idea*, or insight, as it is integrated into the frameworks that we use for understanding and judging what is going on around us. This is a largely unconscious process. Once we consciously explore the experience, we have moved to the stage of *reflection*, where we actively think or talk about what it means to us. In most texts concerned with the assessment of artistic responses, the assumption is that the student then progresses to *creative output*, usually by articulating a personal response. As mentioned in Chapter 6, this could take the form of imaginative or critical writing, but could also be a drawing, a piece of music, or a dance. It is the student's *output* which is normally the focus of attention.

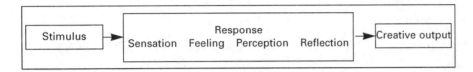

Figure 8.2 *Response continuum*

However, we have noted that many students with special needs will not necessarily be able to produce anything material or performance-based as an outcome. This means that if we want to evaluate the effect of the experience, we must find a way of describing their immediate expressive responses – that is, how they show us that they have engaged with the text. Their responses could form the basis of subsequent creative production, either as an individual or a group activity, but we do not have to depend on an *output* to look at their potential for creativity. We need to start by defining the forms that a response might take. Ross (1978) distinguishes between responses which are purely reactive behaviours, which simply release or give vent to feelings, and responses which are controlled, deliberate and creative, giving form to feeling. 'Reactive expression is about the discharge of tension. Creative expression is about feelings changing and growing' (p. 41).

So, we present our students with an experience, and they respond to it in whatever way they can. At first, students may only be responding reactively, in Ross's terms, but even a reactive response is valuable as a starting point. The forms that response will take will vary, but will always consist of some kind of physical, behavioural signal that we 'read' (see Figure 8.3). The creative output which is represented in the bottom half of the diagram has to come from somewhere, and must originate from the physical and imaginative responses which result from the student's engagement.

How we read those responses – that is, our interpretations of what they mean – depends on what we are looking for. The model presented here (Figure 8.4) focuses on four related perspectives for evaluating an expressive response:

- the *experiential* (engagement /attention)
- the *affective* (feeling)
- the *cognitive* (thinking and language)
- the *aesthetic* (unity of engagement, thinking and feeling)

Immediate personal response

- Body orientation (*tense, relaxed, turned towards or away, slumped or upright* etc.)
- Facial expression
- Vocalisation
- Use of the hands (*reach, touch, throw, pull, push* etc.)
- Movement
- Gestures which represent objects and events
- Signs from a sign language
  British Sign Language, Paget-Gorman Signed Speech, Makaton Vocabulary
- Spoken words

- -

Transforming response into creative output

- Writing
  using conventional text
  using graphic symbols such as Rebus, Makaton, Picture Communication Symbols
- Visual and plastic arts
  drawing, painting, collage, sculpture, textiles
- Music
  singing, use of instruments
- Dance
  choreographed movement
- Drama
  dramatic production

Figure 8.3 *Modes of expressive response*

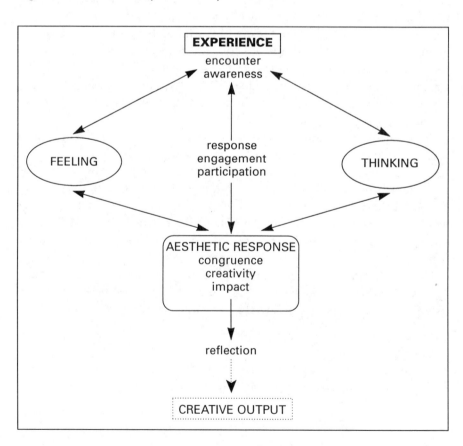

Figure 8.4 *Response to literature: an evaluative framework*

We begin with an evaluation of the level at which the student is reacting to the *experience* – since some level of engagement or attention is a prerequisite to the development of a response. We then consider the two dimensions of *thinking* and *feeling*, based on the notion of dual modes of knowing proposed by Bruner, Gardner and others. The fourth dimension is the *aesthetic*, an integration of experience, thinking and feeling.

Experience

Evaluating what the experience is like involves a focus on the level of the student's engagement with the activity. Teachers and therapists who are asked about how they evaluate responses frequently report monitoring their awareness of whether students are attending, enjoying, and involved with the lesson. Brown (1996) has provided a hierarchical model for evaluating experience, which is adopted for the purposes of our framework (see Figure 8.4a).

```
• encounter – being present, being provided with sensations
• awareness – noticing that something is going on
• response – showing surprise, enjoyment, dissatisfaction
• engagement – directed attention; focused looking, listening; showing
  interest, recognition, recall
• participation – supported participation, sharing, turn-taking
• involvement – active participation, reaching out, joining in, commenting
• achievement – gaining, consolidating, practising skills, knowledge,
  concepts
```

Figure 8.4a *Levels of experience (Brown 1996)*

In relation to the continuum of development of an aesthetic response, *encounter* and *awareness* probably operate at the level of *sensation*, *response*, *engagement*, *participation* and *involvement* represent a stage at which *perceptions* or *ideas* may be developing and the final level of *achievement* is the point at which *reflection* would probably develop.

Feeling

The affective dimension (Figure 8.4b) is concerned with the level and the quality of feelings that the student is enabled to express in response to the experience. Level is used to indicate the extent to which students are able to enter into the experiences of others, engage with them, and grow emotionally in so doing. From studies of affective development we know that infants at first react to the emotions of others, which may be a purely imitative behavioural response. However, the imitation of an expression may be enough to generate the associated feeling: smiling or sadness. From about two years onwards, children acquire and use words to express feelings (like, love, happy, sad), and they not only make associations between predictable events and feelings (e.g. birthdays with pleasure) but seem to understand that other people have feelings which differ from their own. By four years of age, children recognise the mental states and feelings of other people (Baron-Cohen 1993). In the framework used here, there are four levels of development for affective responses:

- *Reaction* – immediate affective response to atmosphere or sensation – laughter and excitement in the battle scene of *Macbeth*, unease with spooky music.
- *Imitation* – showing response to the feelings of others, e.g. imitating someone else's facial expression, joining in with vocalisations.
- *Empathy* – showing some response or awareness of the feelings of others, e.g. by a comment, reaching out to touch someone who is acting (or really) sad.
- *Imaginative empathy* – ability to take on a role; to imagine what someone else (fictional or real) would feel like.

As well as having some idea of the level of response, which is hierarchical, we need to know something about the quality of response at each level. Students may, or may not, be able to talk or write in ways that directly convey their feelings. Here we are concerned more with the quality of the feeling, whether it is nonverbal or verbal, indicating the range, intensity and appropriateness of feelings:

- *Range* – how many different feelings can a person express in different contexts?
- *Intensity* – how involved does the person become in the imaginative experience?
- *Appropriateness* – does the expressed emotion fit with the context? For example, some students may not get beyond the stage of laughing to express release of tension, at the most dramatic moments, but others may be able to control their expressions of mood to suit the atmosphere.

A note on enjoyment

One of the most common questions that teachers seem to ask of students is 'Did you like the story/poem/film?' The purpose of asking it is not always evident, since we do not necessarily have to like an experience (or like everything about an experience) in order to get something out of it. However, it is true to say that this can be a starting point for exploring with the student what they liked (or not) and why. For students with more severe learning difficulties, if they do not enjoy the experience at some level, they may not attend, and therefore are unlikely to learn anything – hence it is important to record evidence of likes and dislikes.

People generally rely on reading facial expressions and body language to determine enjoyment or dislike, with the proviso that if you are working with people who have multiple disabilities, you may mistakenly interpret involuntary facial movements, such as grins or blinks, as indicative of feelings (Green and Reid 1996; Lancioni *et al.* 1996). The responses of some students may be very individual, so that only staff who know them well will be able to determine how they felt about the experience.

To establish preferences for events, objects and activities, the usual approach involves the presentation of two items which are equally familiar. The one which is chosen consistently over time probably represents one which the student likes. Preferences will also be indicated by the extent to which a student is willing to tolerate, or actively join in, an activity.

Thinking

The cognitive dimension is concerned with the students' conceptual and linguistic response to the experience, and draws on the existing framework of

LEVEL		QUALITY	
	Range	Intensity	Appropriateness
Reaction Imitation Empathy Imaginative empathy			

Figure 8.4b Ways of looking at affective responses

the National Curriculum, as well as theories of the development of language functions (Roth and Spekman 1984). We are interested in the student's ability to recall, predict, explain, justify, compare and contrast: in other words, in mental states and the way these are expressed in language (Figure 8.4c). These skills can be summarised as:

- memory (recognition and discrimination)
- thinking
- language.

The starting point is the student's capacity to recognise similarities and differences, since this appears to be fundamental to the way in which infants categorise and attach meaning to experience (Mandler 1992).

Recognition

To establish whether or not students recognise and remember the experience, you can observe their discrimination, anticipation, choice of correct object of reference, moving to habitual place; looking at or picking up an associated object when a piece of music is played as a cue. For example, I was able to infer that Susan, a woman with profound learning difficulties, remembered a drama session when in response to being shown the case for the video cassette we used, she took it, got up and moved to the room where we held the session.

Thinking skills

There are certain key skills, listed in Figure 8.4c, which seem to be involved in accessing all areas of the curriculum: they are mentioned in the documentation for all the main subject areas, such as Maths, Science, History, Geography, Music and Technology. Although most evident in the linguistic responses of pupils (spoken, signed or written), they may also be demonstrated nonverbally – as when pupils solve experimental problems by actually manipulating materials, or in the composition of a piece of music. Pupils may indicate in the way that they interact with others that they are predicting what will happen next, or understand a problem in the context of a story.

- Describing, comparing and contrasting
- Predicting
- Recall and sequencing
- Hypothesising and imagining
- Problem-solving
- Reasoning
- Instructing
- Debating

Figure 8.4c Thinking skills across the curriculum

Language skills

The framework of the English curriculum emphasises the teaching and assessment of pupils' abilities to understand and express themselves linguistically. The aspects which are of interest include:

- *vocabulary and meanings* – the range of concepts available to a student, and the relationships between sets of concepts (e.g. antonyms and synonyms; categories of words such as fruit or furniture).
- *grammar* – the structure of words and sentences.
- *pragmatics* – the appreciation of the way in which language use varies with context.

These can be assessed using the existing framework within the curriculum, educational approaches (e.g. Broadbent 1995) or specific assessments of language and interaction (e.g. Dewart and Summers 1996; Knowles and Masidlover 1982; Locke 1985; Rinaldi 1992; Wiig and Secord 1996).

In the evaluative framework, affect and cognition (feeling and thinking) can be regarded as parallel to each other (see Figure 8.4d).

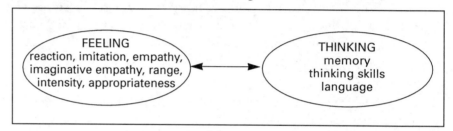

Figure 8.4d *Feeling and thinking*

Aesthetic

Aesthetic judgements are notoriously relative and subjective, yet there is general agreement that aesthetics is concerned with the fitness of form to purpose, artistic creativity, and cultural relevance (Ross 1978; Geertz 1983). The aesthetic aspect of a response is concerned with the integrity of form, thought and feeling in a cultural context. In evaluating the aesthetic quality of a student's response, we can focus on three key aspects:

- *Congruence.* The question here is whether the response fits with the context in a way that strikes us as satisfying or apt. It's a slightly different concept from appropriateness of feeling, which is more to do with social acceptability. Here the aptness lies in the relationship between the form of the student's response and the meaning of the text.
- *Creativity* is defined in this context as an innovation. Does the student's response add anything new to the experience?
- *Impact* refers to the effect of a student's response on the rest of the group. Does it contribute in a way which affects the social context? This relates to Geertz's principle (pp. 12–13) that art is not perceived in isolation, but as part of a network of social and cultural interactions.

The example of Lenny may clarify what is meant by *impact*.

Lenny

Lenny, a stocky young man with Down's syndrome, communicated primarily nonverbally, although he had a small vocabulary of manual signs, which he occasionally combined in two-word sentences. He took part each week in a dramatisation of *The Odyssey* through interactive games (Grove and Park 1996). One activity involved the desertion of the nymph, Calypso, by Odysseus, and involved a paired dance whereby the leaver (Odysseus) slid 'his' hands down the arms of his partner until only fingertips were touching, before turning away. This activity was designed with the needs of people with dual sensory impairment in mind, in the knowledge that loss of a familiar and trusted partner is an all-too-common occurrence in institutions where staff turn-over is high, and leaving rituals are often perfunctory. The dance was envisaged as slow, sad and sexy, using blues as a background. However, for Lenny, the meaning seemed to be different. He was dancing with a staff member whom he rather fancied, and he introduced a sort of twirl as he turned, and a little wave, which was distinctly flirtatious. It had the effect of changing the atmosphere to inject a note of humour.

Lenny's response was not, as it happened, congruent with the atmosphere that we were trying to establish. However, looked at from another perspective, he was contributing his own meaning in a way that did not just affect himself and his partner, but had an impact on the group – that is, we can look at his behaviour, not only for an integrity between form and feeling (which was undoubtedly present) but for a social dimension; the extent to which it contributes to the framing of meaning for the group.

Intentionality

One question which is relevant, particularly for students with profound learning difficulties, is whether a response needs to be intentionally produced in order to qualify under the heading of aesthetic evaluation. Because our approach defines meaning as something that emerges as the product of an interaction, it allows for the contribution of unintentional, 'serendipitous' responses from students to the creative atmosphere of the event.

In fact, of course, debates rage in the art world about whether artistic effects are willed or emerge almost accidentally. When form and function are closely integrated, even accidental brushstrokes can contribute felicitously to the whole. Adrian Searle, reviewing an exhibition of paintings by de Kooning, comments:

> For at least the last 15 years of his life de Kooning suffered from Alzheimer's disease, yet continued to paint even when the progress of the disease meant he couldn't tie his shoelaces or sign his name ... in the last years, before he drifted away, did he mean what he did as a painter? Was he, in effect, still there? The paintings raise all sorts of issues about intention, volition, about painting and about being human ... (*Guardian*, 30 December 1997).

At a more mundane level, by encouraging individuals to expand their horizons through play, we may help to develop creative and spontaneous behaviour.

The following examples of unintended responses were observed during projects which focused on Shakespeare's *Macbeth* in schools for pupils with severe and moderate learning difficulties.

Shezad

Shezad has profound and multiple learning difficulties, with no verbal communication. It must be admitted that for most of the time his realisation of the role of King Duncan was characterised by its half-heartedness. He would lean his chin on his hand, crown sliding over his ear, and stare into the middle distance, unmoved by the devotion of his followers, the battles waged on his behalf, and the wiles of his hostess. However, for some reason, Shezad came to life during the game which dramatised the choice of the Macbeths between good and evil, loyal friendship and murder. This involved each actor confronting Shezad, and being pulled towards a dagger (to the left), or a chalice (to the right) by staff who alternated lines from the play supporting one position or the other: e.g. 'He's here in double trust' (pull to right) 'When you durst do it, then you were a man' (pull to left). As it happens, Shezad is hemiplegic, and can only raise his right hand to reach or point. Actually, I had forgotten this entirely, being absorbed in the logistics of setting the game up, but when he suddenly started shouting loudly and pointing to the right side each time someone was confronted with the choice, I realised that his limited motor skills were being employed to considerable dramatic effect.

Jenny

Jenny also has profound learning difficulties, but was much more engaged in the drama than Shezad. She has no functional hand skills at all, and we monitored her involvement principally by checking her gaze direction and facial expression. She did, however, vocalise, and at the point where we were developing character through various exercises (music and vocalisation), she seemed to imitate a wail for Lady Macbeth by a high pitched, prolonged vocalisation.

Nadia

Nadia's role was Lady Macbeth. Mostly she had to be supported to stand or move, and she rarely made eye contact with anyone, although she frequently smiled. Nadia has Rett's syndrome, a genetic condition which affects cognitive, communicative and motor functioning. One of the most characteristic features of Rett's is obsessive clasping and re-clasping of the hands, often known as hand-washing. Now, 'hand-washing' in Rett's syndrome may not usually be functional (indeed we spend a lot of time trying to substitute more positive alternatives) but it could be argued that the character of Lady Macbeth offers the perfect opportunity to endow this behaviour with meaning, albeit in a very limited way.[1]

In each of these three examples, behaviour which is unintentionally produced by the student is endowed with meaning in the context – that is, we use 'scaffolding' to frame and contextualise the student's response, just as we do in the development of communication with both infants and people functioning at a preverbal level who have learning difficulties (Nind and Hewett 1994; Coupe and Goldbart 1988), or the development of creative writing. At an aesthetic level, the behaviours are *congruent* with the atmosphere of the play. The next examples are of students with rather more linguistic ability, who were able to involve themselves actively in the drama.

Gail

In the scene immediately before Macbeth's murder of Duncan, the students are asked to supply spooky noises that might be heard at night, prior to making the sounds as the two assassins creep towards their goal. Groups of students came up with different ideas – a creaky door; an owl hoot; the wind. One of the students, Gail, had been behaving in a very autistic way during the workshop – wandering across the acting space, twiddling obsessively and apparently failing to notice anything that was going on. However, when her group were asked to volunteer a sound, Gail looked me straight in the eye and produced an eerie 'miaow'. Needless to say, this was the sound which was adopted for their contribution. Gail's contribution was not only congruent, but also creative – she was adding a new element within the framework of the game.

---

[1] It is recognized that this example may be seen as controversial; in fact one arts worker with whom I discussed this approach thought it was highly irresponsible. I offer it because I think it makes for an interesting debate about our responses to disability. We might decide that the risk of reinforcing maladaptive behaviour is too great. Or we might decide that since we can never eradicate the behaviour, this is one context where it will be accepted.

Stephen

Two scenes on, the murder had been carried out, and Macbeth and Lady Macbeth were frantically washing their hands. I was narrating along the lines of 'they had to try to get their hands clean, when *suddenly...*'. I paused fractionally, and Stephen, a student with moderate learning difficulties, interjected without any prompting three loud, peremptory knocks on the bench beside him. Stephen knew the story, since the students had been told it, had watched the video, and had made props before the workshop. His response showed not only that he could recall and sequence the events of the story, but that he could produce a dramatic effect which was aesthetically congruent. Stephen was not really innovating – he was reproducing something he had heard and seen in the correct place in the story, but what he did do was to enhance the meaning and raise the general level of engagement of the group. In that sense, he made a powerful *impact* on the social context of the interaction – there was no doubt that the rest of the audience really responded to his action.

As an illustration of how the model might operate, let us work through the example of Jenny's 'Lady Macbeth wail'.

The model in operation

Experience

Observation of Jenny's behaviour suggested that she was definitely engaged for most of the session, since she watched what was going on, smiled and produced excited vocalisations.

Her *participation* had to be supported by Eddie, the assistant who was holding her throughout, but as stated, the fact that her cry immediately followed on from my model suggests that she may have been echoing it.

Affect

Jenny's vocalisations, as stated, seemed to convey mainly excitement. She can express pain and discomfort, and pleasure through low vocalisations at other points. She has little control of facial muscles, and although we tend to interpret her smile as indicating enjoyment, it may at times be reflex. Her wail, however, had a distinctly melancholy quality to it. In subsequent sessions, therefore, we might look to see if we can get Jenny to reproduce this quality (we might also play with different sounds in a music session). In terms of the level of expression of affect, Jenny seems to be functioning mainly *reactively*, although she may be able to *imitate*.

Thinking and language

Jenny is operating at a preverbal level, and mainly reacts to stimuli, though she does at times show evidence of anticipation. Her contingent vocalisation suggests the potential for imitation. We might want to see if in subsequent sessions when we are working with Lady Macbeth's sound, Jenny can reproduce her cry, or introduce it spontaneously.

Aesthetics

The sound Jenny produced definitely showed *congruence*: it was appropriate to the atmosphere, and to the character. Although it may represent a new departure for Jenny, it was an imitation rather than an *innovation*. As far as the *impact* goes, it was not clear whether the other students were aware of the quality of the sound, although I picked up on it and commented. We would want to see if subsequently, Jenny's sound could help to build a social meaning for the group which conveyed something of the character of Lady Macbeth.

Summary

A four-dimensional model is proposed for the evaluation of the expressive response: the level at which the student engages with the experience; the feelings which are expressed; the thinking and language processes which are evident; and the aesthetic dimension, which is concerned with the quality of the form of the response and its social implications. The approach offers a way of thinking coherently about behaviours which we often recognise to be exciting, or unexpected, or spontaneous, but that we can only note as anecdotes in the absence of a structured framework. If we cannot define what is significant about these behaviours, there is a risk that they will be undervalued and ignored, particularly by the people who are currently obsessed with outcomes:

> ... such people usually attempt only to assess those aspects of education which seem to lend themselves to precise measurement, and that other aspects become victims of what might be called the 'disappearance by default' syndrome - the notion that what can't be measured doesn't exist – and vanish in a kind of educational 'Bermuda Triangle'! (Goodman 1981, p. 55)

There are various ways in which the framework may be applied:

- to contribute to a profile of students, by describing their affective and creative potential;
- as a basis for developing some form of creative output – dance, drama, artwork, music or writing. The framework provides continuity between students who can only respond expressively, and those who can move into creative production. It also allows for continuity between creative arts subjects in the curriculum.
- to support progression for individual pupils. By focusing on key aspects of their responses, we may enable them to develop a greater range or depth of engagement, feeling and aesthetic contribution.
- as a way of capturing the significance of responses by people with profound learning difficulties, which are often fleeting and intermittent.

There is no need to work through all aspects of the model for every student. It is up to the teacher to decide what is important to evaluate for particular students in particular lessons. For example, you may want to focus on the way a student uses language in different lessons – so the focus would be on the cognitive dimension. Or you may only want to get a measure of the student's level of engagement, in which case you will look at the levels of experience.

Other frameworks will also be useful – for example, if the student's response is primarily through dance, art or music, you could use the assessment tools which are recommended in the relevant National Curriculum documents, and other texts in the Curriculum for All series, such as *Music for All* (Wills and Peter 1996); *Drama for All* (Peter 1994); *Art for All* (Peter 1996); and *Dance for All* (Allen and Coley 1996).

POSTSCRIPT

> The parent helps the child discover what may be done with its lips and its limbs. This is the first poetry.
>
> (James Fenton, *The Manila Manifesto*, 1993)

When Keith Park and I embarked on *Odyssey Now* (I fear the pun is inescapable), we met with considerable scepticism, and sometimes wondered if we were on the right tack. Later, we wrote of the need to take risks and make mistakes (Grove and Park 1997) in the pursuit of imaginative approaches to developing language and communication, that would sustain us as well as our students. It has been the enthusiastic response of practitioners – teachers and speech and language therapists – and the students themselves, which has convinced us that it is sometimes worth sailing close to the wind, for the sheer excitement of the experience.

This book also takes some risks. I am aware that to some readers, the interpretations I have placed on some of the responses of my students may seem to credit them with unwarranted awareness and insight. This is not my intention. Rather, I am trying to find a framework and a register to convey the magic intensity of a moment when one connects for an instant with the mind of a person with profound learning difficulties, and recognises the contribution he or she can make to a shared experience. At a fundamental level, we participate as equals in a communicative exchange, and all communication, each look or smile or gesture or word, is unique, is generative, is a fragment of a poem. Even inarticulate lives have a story to tell, as the work of Tim and Wendy Booth remind us (1996). Language is still language, still innately creative, even when it is restricted by a learning difficulty, or shattered and re-formed after an acquired injury. Chris Ireland, who has expressive aphasia resulting from a stroke, is determined to own her language, rather than attempt to force herself into a straitjacket of others' expectations. As a result her writing has a power and energy to which we might all aspire:

> This book belong to the people who tell their stories. Also it belongs with you – the readers to reflect their own experiences and learn and share various perceptions. Living with aphasia is facing daily struggle – pain, confusions, isolating, anxiety – and learning, and understanding within the social world – so noisy, so stressful, so dirty polluted, needy, greedy. But some care, some are open to learn, and some have vision. (Ireland 1997)

These words are as applicable to the lives of children and adults with learning difficulties as to those with aphasia. Sharing literature in all its forms may open a window into different worlds – the grimpen moor conjured up by Jane Grecic, the caves where Gollum lurks in Caroline Fyfe's version of *The Hobbit*, or an old ship, creaking into life again as the rowers pick up their oars and make for enchanted islands.

APPENDIX 1

Examples of poetry

The following are suggestions only, not a definitive list. Some of these poems fall into more than one category, of course, which is a bonus.

Simplicity. Language which can be readily understood, with simple sentence construction and a lot of basic vocabulary.
Grace Nichols *Sea Timeless*
H. H. Munro *Overheard on a Salt Marsh*
Charles Causley *What Has Happened To Lulu?*
Robert Frost *Stopping by Woods on a Snowy Evening*
Anon *This Is the Key of the Kingdom*

Concreteness. Descriptive language referring to sensory experiences which can be illustrated by real examples or pictures.
John Keats *The Eve of St. Agnes*
Adrian Mitchell *Giving Potatoes*
E.E.Cummings *maggie and molly and milly and may*
James Berry *Sunny Market Song*
Mary Hoberman *Yellow Butter*
Christina Rossetti *Goblin Market*
William Carlos Williams *This Is Just To Say*
Maya Angelou *Woman Work*

Rhythm and sound. Language which is strongly patterned, conveying meaning through sound and sense. Onomatopoeia is the technical term for words with in-built sound effects (eg. 'moo', 'splat', 'tee-hee', 'pitter-patter'). This poetry can be readily illustrated by sounds or music, using contrasts between vowels and consonants; short sounds and long sounds; hard sounds and soft sounds.
Anon *The Ballad of Casey Jones*
Alfred Tennyson *The Lotus-Eaters; The Splendour Falls on Castle Walls*
G.K. Chesterton *Lepanto*
John Masefield *Cargoes*
Kit Wright *Red Boots On*
James Berry *Diggin Sing*
T.S. Eliot *Skimbleshanks the Railway Cat*
W.H. Auden *Night Mail*
Eleanor Farjeon *Cat*

Repetition. Language which builds up meaning through repeated sequences and refrains (e.g. traditional folk and fairy tales, songs and ballads).
Anon *The Strange Guest*
Dylan Thomas *Do not go gentle into that good night*
Anon *Lord Randal*
Edward Lear *The Jumblies*

Dramatic language. Language which conveys character, or narrative, and can be illustrated through acting, exaggerated for emphasis.
Robert Browning *The Pied Piper of Hamelin*
Samuel Taylor Coleridge *Rime of the Ancient Mariner*
Vachel Lindsay *Daniel Jazz*
Anon *The Ballad of Frankie and Johnnie*
Lord Macauley *The Keeper of the Bridge*
W.H. Auden *The Quarry*
Mike Rosen *Hot Food; The Chocolate Cake*
W.B. Yeats *The Cap and Bells*

Principles of translation into graphic symbols and signs

Tina Detheridge and Nicola Grove

Symbols are graphic representations for ideas, objects or actions. They have been used as part of written communication systems for centuries. Egyptian hieroglyphs are perhaps the most well known. We use symbols in our environment today to convey meaning efficiently and quickly – without having to read more complex text. Symbols have been used for many years to support people with communication difficulties as a means of indicating what they wish to communicate. More recently they have been used to provide significant support for written material for non-text readers. The following section provides a brief overview of symbols and the issues surrounding their use as a means of providing support for accessing literature and as a tool for facilitating non-text writers to become authors.

Symbols

There is a spectrum of graphic representations which can be used to transmit elements of language. At one end there are pictures. Pictures are usually used to convey an amalgam of ideas rather than linguistic elements.

In the middle range of the spectrum are pictorial symbols, normally simple line drawings, which are created to represent single ideas or concepts. At the other end of the spectrum are abstract symbols which are more conceptual in essence. Blissymbolics comprises a number of basic elements which can be compounded to create new meanings. For example the pictorial symbol and Bliss symbol for trousers are:

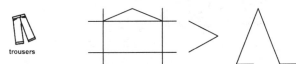

Figure A1 *Rebus trousers, Blissymbolics trousers*

The Bliss compound describes trousers by function – cloth which goes on the legs – the pictorial symbol gives a drawing of trousers, whilst the picture will show a specific pair of trousers, and possibly someone wearing them. It is clear to see from this illustration, that whilst the more abstract system is capable of great linguistic flexibility, the conceptual understanding may also be complex. A person with a learning difficulty may be more likely to learn and remember pictorial symbols.

There are a number of dilemmas in the use of pictorial symbols which need careful thought if the relationship between the images and the meaning is to be satisfactory. At the most basic level the text is the dominant communication, and each word is separately supported by a symbol.

Figure A2   *The dog eats a bone.*

In this type of communication it is important to select an image which represents the context of the word. It is quite possible to have a range of images for a word, each representing a different meaning.

Figure A3   Go back home   Go back home

Some words, such as the majority of nouns and verbs, can easily be represented by a graphic symbol. Other concepts adhere to certain conventions. For example the generic building symbol is used as the root for a range of buildings.

Figure A4   library, hospital, bank, school

Time related vocabulary uses a vertical line to represent the current time giving rise to a series of symbols such as

Figure A5   before, at, after, until, continue, from

The more pictorial symbols are generally easy to recognise, but the symbols for these more abstract concepts need to be learned in just the same way as written words. Some pictorial symbols are made as compounds, which again may vary in the ease with which they can be immediately recognised or need to be learned.

Figure A6   transport, animals, confident

The final group are those items which cannot be represented pictorially, such as *if, is, but, sorry*. These can only be represented by fairly arbitrary abstract symbols. Not all readers will be able to remember and understand the use of these items, and it may be more appropriate to consider representing the meaning graphically by focusing only on the key-information carrying words. The relationship between the text and the symbol communication should ideally be considered carefully for each potential reader. This concerns the relative sizes of text and graphic as well as the selection of words which are supported.

Readers who can manage some text but need some help may prefer a display which has large text and small symbols. Or the reader may be mainly a text reader, but require help with specific vocabulary, which can be symbolised. Other readers, who look principally at the symbols, may prefer larger symbols and smaller text. While for some readers it may be more appropriate to switch off some of the small less important words to make the display less cluttered, but still convey the essential concepts.

Not all concepts and meanings can easily be represented by pictorial symbols. The exact words and intentions will dictate this. Consider for example these two poems:

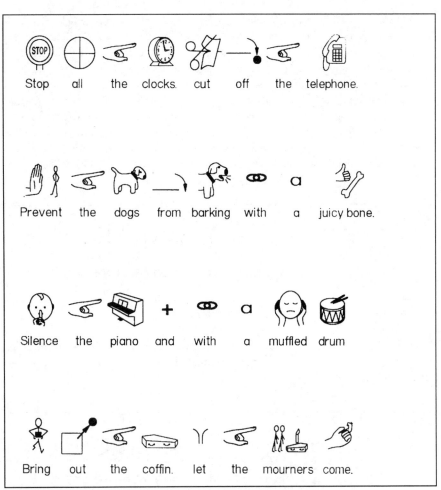

Figure A7 Funeral Blues, *W.H. Auden*

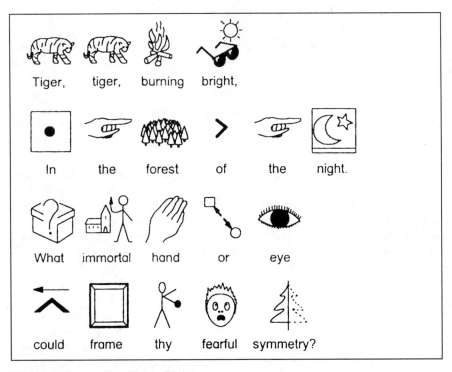

Figure A8 The Tiger, *Blake*

The Auden has very straightforward concepts which can be represented quite easily by concrete symbols, whereas the concepts in the last two lines of the Blake are very difficult and do not lend themselves to such visual representation. No doubt a conceptual meaning could be constructed, but the meaning may not be any more accessible through this medium than it is in orthographic script.

There is one particular difficulty relating to the use of symbols with poetry which needs consideration. If the poetry is essentially an aural medium and the text words are the prompts to the sound of the words, it can be argued that the symbols chosen also need to prompt the appropriate spoken word, which may not necessarily be the most appropriate symbol visually. A typical example is the word 'before'. This will normally have a temporal meaning, but Shakespeare used it spatially:

Figure A9 (i)   *Is this a dagger I see before me?*

This will prompt the correct words, but technically the sense of 'before' is incorrect, being used in a spatial sense rather than temporal. More appropriate might be the spatial symbol.

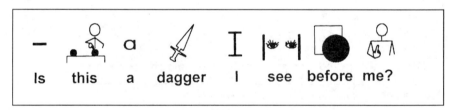

Figure A9 (ii)   *Is this a dagger I see before me?*

The sense here is correct, but introduces a possible confusion with the preposition 'in front'. Another alternative is to omit part of the sentence, and use only the symbols for 'Is this a dagger?'

There are no rights and wrongs in this situation. It will require the sensitive intervention of the teacher, who will need to decide what is more important in any context. For example, if the symbols are being used to cue recall of the text, if a pupil is reading a poem in assembly, then the symbol for 'before' will be better than the symbol for 'in front of'.

The real difficulty with symbols of any type being used to prompt words or sounds rather than conceptual meanings is that there is not always a single word/sound linked to the image, and whilst we will accept the slightly less common or ambiguous use of the word 'before' in text and spoken word, we could have difficulty when the graphic removes the ambiguity or triggers a different word. It is likely that the most successful use of symbols as a means of giving access to spoken literature is as a prompt to the sounds or to whole ideas rather than as a prompt to individual word meanings.

Signs   The issues involved in translating from text to sign are similar to the issues associated with graphic symbols. In a literal word to sign approach, the words are translated in their original order, but this may result in a less direct and meaningful realisation than if the meaning is put directly into sign. For example, in the following extract from

Macbeth, the first part of the conversation translates easily into sign. However, Lady Macbeth's final words are metaphorical, and of the three possible versions, the third is probably the clearest.

Original text	Possible sign versions
Macbeth: My dearest love Duncan comes here tonight.	MY LOVE KING D COME TONIGHT
Lady Macbeth: And when goes hence?	WHEN GO?
Macbeth: Tomorrow, as he purposes	TOMORROW SAME HE THINK
Lady Macbeth: Oh never Shall sun that morrow see!	a. NEVER SUN DAY SEE b. SUNRISE NEVER c. TOMORROW NEVER

Certain principles of the language should ideally be respected in word to sign translation. The grammar of sign dictates that you should remember where your sign for COME originated when you sign TOMORROW SAME HE THINK, and make sure to sign HE in that location. This tells the viewer that it is the same person coming (Duncan) who is thinking of leaving tomorrow. In option a., the sign for SEE should be angled down from the position of SUN towards the position of DAY, indicating that SUN is the subject of the verb, and DAY is the object.

Note also that the visual logic of sign language makes it more appropriate to put NEVER at the end of the sequence rather than at the beginning, because an entity needs to be established in space before it is negated.

Sign language also has individual formal properties which create visual dynamic patterns which are important in poetry. In version c., the BSL sign for SUN is the same as LIGHT, made at eye level. The hand opens out in a short movement down and toward the signer, so that the fingers are spread and pointed. The pointed finger of the sign SEE which follows has a visual echo of SUN in its handshape. If you are going to sign a poem or story, it is a good idea to rehearse it a few times in front of a mirror, so that you can see which combinations of signs work best.

If you know some vocabulary, but are unfamiliar with the structure of sign language, do not be too worried. As with symbols, you may choose to translate only a few key words into sign – just keep the meaning clear and comprehensible to your students. The Dictionary of British Sign Language is an invaluable source for sign translation. However, do not be seduced into thinking that you always have to find the exact and specific sign; it may be more appropriate to use the vocabulary with which individuals are familiar. For example, although there is a BSL sign for *still*, the refrain from *The Strange Guest* can be signed as follows:

And still she sat, and still she reeled	SIT, REEL (to *reel* is to *spin*, so you can draw the outline of a spinning wheel in the air)
And still she wished for company	WANT FRIEND

In conclusion, whether you are planning to translate into sign or into symbol, the most important thing to remember is to give some thought before you start to the meaning of the text, the role of the translation, and the needs of your students.

Brien, D. (Ed.) 1992. *Dictionary of British Sign Language.* London: Faber and Faber/ British Deaf Association.

APPENDIX 3

Teaching resources

Most of the resources listed here are aimed at mainstream, as there is very little currently available which takes account of the needs of pupils with severe problems in language and communication. You are strongly recommended to obtain copies on sale or return, and consider whether the resource is appropriate for you. Sometimes you will find that the frameworks are useful, and the ideas can be adapted.

Storytelling

Aylwin, T. *Traditional Storytelling and Education*. Available from 13, Red Hill, Chislehurst, Kent BR7 6DB (includes a directory of storytellers).

Colwell, E. (1980) *Storytelling*. London: Bodley Head.

Howe, A. and Johnson, J. (eds) (1992) *Storytelling in the Classroom*. London: Hodder and Stoughton.

Maddern, E. (1992) *A Teacher's Guide to Storytelling at Historic Sites*. English Heritage.

Powling, C. (1997) *Storytelling in the Classroom*. Reading and Language Information Centre: Reading, Berks.

Rosen, B. (1988) *And None of it was Nonsense: the Power of Storytelling in School*. MGP Publications: Glasgow.

Zipes, J. (1995) *Creative Storytelling*. London: Routledge.

Video

Barton, B. (1993) *Story matters video: a guide to storytelling in the classroom*. Shows a well-known storyteller in action in the classroom, and discussing techniques with teachers. Centre for Language in Primary Education.

Shakespeare

Gibson, R. (1998) *Teaching Shakespeare: a Handbook for Teachers*. Cambridge: Cambridge University Press.

Gibson, R. (1997) *Shakespeare's Language*: photocopiable worksheets. Cambridge: Cambridge University Press.

Gilmour, M. (ed.) (1997) *Shakespeare for All in Primary Schools*. London: Cassell.

Gilmour, M. (ed.) (1997) *Shakespeare for All in Secondary Schools*. London: Cassell.

Reynolds, P. (1991) *Practical Approaches to Teaching Shakespeare*. Oxford: Oxford University Press.

Teaching stories

Mellor, B., Raleigh, M. and Ashton, P. (1984) *Making Stories*. English and Media Centre.

Mellor, B., Hemming, J. and Leggett, J. (1984) *Changing Stories*. English and Media Centre.

Two books with ideas for organising the writing of stories.

Broadbent, S. (1995) *Key Stage 3 English Units*. English and Media Centre. Photocopiable activities for a range of literature.

Graham, J. (1997) *Cracking Good Books: Teaching Literature at Key Stage 2*. Sheffield: National Association for the Teaching of English.
Teacher notes and pupil activities for 24 stories and poems by well-known children's authors.

Redfern, A. (1994) *Starting with Story Series for Early Years*. Scholastic Publications.
Themes and ideas for activities at Key Stage 1. May be adapted for older pupils.

Sedgwick, F. (1990) *Teaching Children's Literature in the Primary School*. London: David Fulton Publishers.

Dorling Kindersley Classics series: *Legend of Robin Hood, Black Beauty, Dracula, Hunchback of Notre Dame*.

Dracula
Education pack + CD of score from the Northern Ballet Theatre, West Park Centre, Spen Lane, Leeds, LS16 5BE.
The pack traces the development of Northern Ballet's production of *Dracula*. It has many ideas for translating the novel into visual and kinetic images.

The Roald Dahl Club Great Big Box (1998)
Fact file, story cassette, things to make and do relating to Dahl's story books.
The Roald Dahl Teacher Pack (1998)
Activities for 25 class projects, posters and an audiocassette.
Available from the Roald Dahl Club, PO Box 3210, Sherborne, Dorset DT9 4YX. Tel 01935-817163.

Randle, D. (1997) *The Iron Man*. NATE.
A pack of activities with a teacher's guide, related to the story.

BBC Education produce a number of resources for teaching literature – again with a very mainstream focus, but with adaptable ideas. These include *Perspectives on Pride and Prejudice, Doorway to Dickens, Screening Middlemarch, Little Lord Fauntleroy* and *Dead Man's Chest* (pack on Robert Louis Stevenson).
BBC Educational Publishing, PO Box 50, Wetherby, W. Yorkshire LS23. 7E2 Tel 01937-840206

Armstrong, L. and Goddard, A. (1996) *Key Stage 3 Writing*. NATE.
A pack which provides ideas for developing writing skills across a range of abilities.

Wray, D. and Lewis, M. (1997) *Practical Ways to Teach Reading for Information*. Reading and Language Information Centre.

Wray, D. and Lewis, M. (1997) *Writing Frames: Scaffolding Children's Non-fiction Writing in a Range of Genres*. Reading and Language Information Centre.

Helpful practical strategies to support children's reading for information, which can be adapted for fiction, and for pupils with difficulties in language and reading.

Resources for particular stories

Reading and writing skills

Teaching poetry

These are inspiring texts for mainstream pupils – but the ideas and the philosophy can be generalised across the range of ability.

Brownjohn, S. (1994) *To Rhyme or not to Rhyme? Teaching Children to Write Poetry.* London: Hodder and Stoughton.
Koch, K. (1990) *'Rose, where did you get that red?' Teaching Great Poetry to Children.* Vintage Books.
Mort, L. (1991) *Starting with Rhyme Series for Early Years.* Scholastic Publications.

Balaam, J. and Merrick, B. (1987) *Exploring Poetry 5–8.* NATE.
Merrick, B. (1991) *Exploring Poetry 8–13.* NATE.
These two books provide a selection of poetry and detailed ideas for their use.

Barrs, M. and Ellis, S. (1995) *Hands on Poetry.* Centre for Language in Primary Education.
Based on a BBC radio series, suggestions for developing children's understanding of poetry through drama, discussion, music, art and other activities.

Pirie, J. (1997) *On Common Ground.* 2nd Edition. WorldWide Fund for Nature.
Pirie, J. (1997) *Apple Fire: the Halesworth School Anthology.* Bloodaxe.
Sedgwick, F. (1997) *Read my Mind: Young Children, Poetry and Learning.* London: Routledge.

Poetry Collections

Folens Poetry Books – have teaching ideas alongside the poetry selections. A variety of titles available from Folens Publishing, Dunstable.

The Nation's 100 Favourite poems (book and cassette) (1996) London: BBC Books.

Heaney, S. and Hughes, T. (1992) *The Rattle Bag.* London: Faber.
Heaney, S. and Hughes, T. (1997) *The School Bag.* London: Faber.

Rosen, M. (ed.) (1991) *The Kingfisher Book of Children's Poetry.* London: Kingfisher.

Bleiman, B. (1995) *The Poetry Pack.* English and Media Centre, 136 Chalton St. London NW1 1RX (with accompanying video of poets and actors reading poems).

Powling, C. and Styles, M. *A Guide to Children's Poetry 0–13.* Reading and Language Information Centre: Reading, Berks.

Douglas, J. (1996) *Poems Deep and Dangerous.* Anthology for mixed ability groups aged 14 and up. Cambridge University Press.

Look, No Hands. Audiotape of James Berry reading his own poetry, with musical background. Available from the Centre for Language in Primary Education.

Texts with adaptations for pupils with special needs

Romeo and Juliet, Macbeth, A Midsummer Night's Dream. Cutting Edge Publications, 26 Haytor Drive, Milber, Newton Abbot, South Devon TQ12 4DU.

Danny the Champion of the World, Shakespeare for All packs. (*Romeo and Juliet, Julius Caesar, A Midsummer Night's Dream*).
All available from: Questions Publishing, 27 Frederick St., Hockley, Birmingham.

94

The Graphic Shakespeare Series: Julius Casear, Romeo and Juliet, Macbeth.
Retold by Hilary Burningham. Evans Brothers.

Simplified text with illustrations, aimed at pupils with limited reading ability, or with English as a second language.

Grove, N. and Park, K. (1996) *Odyssey Now.* London: Jessica Kingsley.
A multisensory approach to the story of Homer's *Odyssey,* designed to develop communication skills for students with severe and profound learning difficulties.

Park, K. and Grove, N. (forthcoming) *Macbeth in Mind.*
Uses Shakespeare's *Macbeth* as a context for developing skills in social cognition for students with a range of learning difficulties.

Park, K. and Grove, N. (forthcoming) *Romeo and Juliet: Multisensory Approaches.* Bag Books.
Fyfe, C. (forthcoming) *The Hobbit: a Multisensory Approach.* Bag Books.
Two short publications which suggest ways of dramatising these stories with students who have severe and profound learning disabilities.

Bag Books – tactile stories for pupils with sensory impairments. 60 Waltham Grove, London SW6 1QR. Bag Books are collections of materials around which individual narratives are developed – plenty of touch, smell and sound cues which you present in a sequence.

Pearson, A. and Aloysius, C. (1994) *The Big Foot: Museums and Children with Learning Difficulties.* British Museum Publications.
Packed with ideas about how to introduce children with special needs to museum trips, which could be integrated in projects on stories or poetry.

CD Roms

BBC Multimedia Shakespeare. CD Roms for *Hamlet, Julius Caesar, The Tempest, Romeo and Juliet, A Midsummer Night's Dream* and *Macbeth.* Collins Educational: FREEPOST, GW 2446, Bishopriggs, Glasgow G64 1BR. Tel. 0141-306-3484/fax 3750 quote code 3309.

Living Classics series. Europress, Europa House, Adlington Park, Macclesfield, SK10 4NP 01625-855000 (includes *Alice in Wonderland, Tom Sawyer, Peter Pan*).

Broderbund Living Books. 0161-477-4235.
Pippi Longstocking. The Cat in the Hat.

Audiotape

See Hear! a Guide to Audiovisual Resources in the Primary School. Reading and Language Information Centre: Reading, Berks.
Covers audio and video cassettes, multimedia, pictures and photo books, slides.
Versions of books, plays and poetry, available on several labels.

Computer software

Speaking for myself
Topologika software in co-operation with the Down's Syndrome Association. For ACORN, RISC OS and PC.
Designed to promote language and literacy, with Rebus symbols, and Makaton signs.
There is a collection of 2–3 word stories, and animated nursery rhymes.

Storymaker. Allows you to create animated speaking stories with sounds. Available from APA, PO Box 59 Tewkesbury, GL20 6AB.

Living Books series. Random House, Iona Software. From TAG 01474-537886.

Writing with Symbols available from Widgit Software, 102 Radford Rd., Leamington Spa, CV31 1LF. Subscribers can receive sets of symbol stories specially created for young people with learning difficulties.

Artists in Residence

If you are interested in having a writer in residence to work alongside your pupils, look at: Sharp, C. and Dust, K. (1997) *Artists in Schools*. Windsor: NFER.

Contact: The Arts Council of England, 14 Great Peter St., London SW1P 3NQ.

Arts Council of Wales, 9 Museum Place, Cardiff CF1 3NX.

Scottish Arts Council, 12 Manor Place, Edinburgh EH3 7DD.

The Arts Council of Northern Ireland, 185 Stranmills, Belfast BT9 5DU.

National Association of Writers in Education. PO Box 1, Sheriff Hutton, York YO6 7YU.

Organisations

The Poetry Society, 22 Betterton St., London WC2H 9BU.

The Poetry Library, Level 5, Royal Festival Hall.
A huge library of modern poetry resources, including magazines, videos and audio cassettes, posters, pictures. Membership is free.

Society for Storytelling, PO Box 2344, Reading RG5 7FG. Tel. 0118-9351381.

The Crick-Crack Club, Interchange Studios, Dalby St., London NW5 3NQ.

National Association for the Teachers of English (NATE), 50 Broadfield Road, Sheffield, S8 OXJ. Conferences, journal, publications and network of teachers.

The English and Media Centre, 136 Chalton St., London NW1 1RX
publish a wide range of resources to support the teaching of English in mainstream schools.

Centre for Language in Primary Education (CLPE), Webber St., London SE1 8QW. Tel. 0171-401-3382
Extensive library of literature, reading programmes, teachers' books on language and literacy, audio and videotapes and educational software. email: clpe@rmplc.co.uk
Admission is by subscription to the journal *Language Matters*.

Reading and Language Information Centre, University of Reading, Bulmershe Court, Earley, Reading, RG6 1HY. Resources to support reading, writing and language in the classroom.

REACH: The National Resource Centre for Children with Reading Difficulties.
Wellington House, Wellington Road, Wokingham, RG40 2AG. 0118-989-1101.
Advice and resources to support access to reading for children with reading, language

and communication problems. They will deal with individual enquiries from professionals and parents, and produce a range of helpful basic leaflets.

The Federation of Children's Book Groups is a national voluntary organisation concerned with children and their books. Liaises with schools, libraries, playgroups and provides a meeting place for parents, librarians, teachers and writers. Local groups, conferences, Children's Book Award, other events related to literature and storytelling, magazine Carousel, newsletters. Advice, inspiration and a chance to meet likeminded lovers of books.
FCBG, 9 West Royd, Pudsey, West Yorks, LS28 8HZ.

Bookpeople are a mailorder company selling discounted books. 01942-723333.

Magazines and journals

Literacy and Learning. Questions Publishing. Lots of practical ideas and resources.

Language Matters. Journal of the Centre for Language in Primary Education. Articles by teachers writing about their practice.

English in Education. NATE journal.
The English and Media Magazine, English and Media Centre
These two journals publish articles, poems and reviews on all aspects of English teaching.

Web sites

Globe Theatre http://www.rdg.ac.uk/globe

BBC Education http://www.bbc.co.uk/education
offers the BBC Learning Station, with TV linked literacy.

BBC Education http://www.bbc.co.uk/education/webguide
for information on subject areas.

Channel 4: www.channel4.co.uk
teaching notes to support schools programmes.

Reading and Language Information Centre,
http://www.rdg.ac.uk/AcaDepts/eh/ReadLang/home.html

Widgit Software
http://www.widgit.com/

Children's literature web guide. www.acs.ucalgary.ca/~dkbrown/index/html
Canadian site with masses of information on children's books and storytelling, links to literacy projects.

APPENDIX 4

Framework for analysis of narrative production

Reprinted from: M. Allen, M. Keroty, J. Sherblom, J. Pettit (1994) 'Children's narrative productions: A comparison of personal event and fictional stories' *Applied Psycholinguistics*, **15**, 149-176

APPENDIX 4.1

DESCRIPTIONS OF PERSONAL EVENT CUE CARDS
1. Playing a trick on someone.
2. Going to the doctor.
3. Playing in the snow.
4. Getting into trouble.
5. Having a tantrum during a shopping trip.
6. A car accident.
7. Being in the hospital.
8. Pets.
9. Being punished by a parent.
10. Friends not sharing a game.
11. Being mad at a friend.
12. Fighting with siblings.
13. Causing an accident while playing.
14. A scary ride in an amusement park.
15. Getting a bandaid put on a cut.

DESCRIPTION OF STORY SEQUENCE CARDS
Costumes
1. Three children find a trunk.
2. They open the trunk and start taking out costumes.
3. As they try on the costumes, a dog peers through the doorway.
4. Fully dressed in costumes, the children turn around. The dog gets scared and runs away.

Boy painting picture
1. A boy paints a picture while a bird is perched on the edge of a paint jar.
2. The bird steps in paint and walks across a sidewalk in the picture, leaving bird prints.
3. The boy seems upset and shows picture to an adult woman (mother or teacher).
4. The woman hangs up the picture and both seem to be admiring it.

APPENDIX 4.2

Story Grammar Categories	*Description*
Setting(s)	Internal states, external states, or habitual actions that serve to introduce the characters and the social and physical environment. *Example:* He had a pet bird he could pull out of a cage.
Initiating Events (IE)	Natural occurrences, actions, or environmental states resulting from actions. *Example:* The bird stepped in the paint.
Motivating States (MS)	Internal states, such as affects, cognitions, or goals, that motivate the protagonist. *Example:* The boy got sad.
Attempts (A)	Actions initiated by an event or a motivating state that are preparatory to goal attainment. *Example:* So he went to his mother to show her what he did.
Consequences (C)	Actions that directly achieve, or fail to achieve, a goal; existing states once all attempts have failed; or the effect of a cause-and-effect relation. *Example:* And she said, "That could be a bird that was walking just for a walk."
Reactions (R)	Internal states precipitated by the events, attempts, or consequences that do not motivate behavior; or purposeless actions that are precipitated by events, attempts, or consequences. *Example:* And then he said, "That's a good idea."

APPENDIX 4.3

Narrative Structural Patterns	*Description*
No Structure (NS)	Animate character, but no temporal or causal relations or continued sequence of events.
Descriptive Sequence (DS)	Describes character(s), surroundings, and habitual actions with no causal relationships. Three or more statements connected by additive relations. *Missing:* action sequences, causal relations; goal, plan, and consequence.
Action Sequence (AS)	A list of three or more actions that are temporally rather than causally ordered. *Missing:* causal relations; goal, plan, and consequence.
Reactive Sequence (RS)	A set of changes that automatically cause other changes with no planning involved. These usually consist of settings, initiating events, and consequence. *Missing:* goal, plan, attempt.
Simple Episode (SE)	An initiating event or internal response of a main character occurs and is followed by a consequence. A goal or intention either may or may not be stated, but it can be inferred. These episodes usually consist of settings, initiating events or a motivating state, and a consequence. *Missing:* plan, attempt, obstacle.
Complete Episode (CE)	A complete episode consists of an obligatory consequence statement plus setting, and at least two of the following three statements: initiating event, motivating state, and attempt.
Incomplete Episode (ICE)	All components of a complete, simple, or complex episode may be present, except the requisite consequence.

APPENDIX 4.4

SAMPLE SCORED TRANSCRIPTS

Subject 37, age 6;4

Fictional story: A multiple-episode story consisting of a simple episode (lines 1-2) linearly connected to a complete episode (lines 3-13).

MS&S	1.	Once upon a time, there was a boy who wanted to paint a picture.
C	2.	So he painted one.
S	3.	Then he had a pet bird he could pull out of a cage but he wouldn't get lost and go outside.
S	4.	So the bird was looking at the boy paint his picture.
IE	5.	And when the boy wasn't looking, the bird stepped in the ink.
IE	6.	And then when the little boy was painting, the bird stepped on the sidewalk.
MS	7.	And he got a little sad.
MS&AT	8.	The boy got sad so he went to his mother to show her what he did.
C	9.	And she said, "That could just be a bird that was walking (and) just for a walk."
R	10.	And then he said, "That's a good idea."
C	11.	And he smiled.
R	12.	And he gave it to her to hang up.
R	13.	And they lived happily ever after.

Subject 9, age 5;3

Personal experience: A complete-episode story consisting of a reactive sequence (lines 1–3) functioning as an initiating event embedded in a complete episode (lines 1–5).

		Can you tell me about what happened to yours [paper reindeer]?
		How did you cut it out and what happened to the antlers?
IE	1.	Well, my black reindeer just came running up.
S	2.	The white reindeer was right here [points into space].
C	3.	"Poooosch," and he knocked his antlers off.
		And then what happened?
AT&C	4.	I tried to staple them back on but it didn't work.
R	5.	And then you came.

Subject 2, age 4;11

Personal experience: A reactive sequence.

		I've been on one of those.
		A roller coaster? Can you tell me about it?
S	1.	It's just a short ride.
		What happened?
IE	2.	I went down a scary road, that thing.
C	3.	I felt dizzy.
		You felt dizzy?
R	4.	And then my Mom (first there was a big ride and) she like me.

ACKNOWLEDGMENTS

We thank Mary Marin for her assistance in scoring the transcripts. Without the enthusiastic support and participation of the Montessori and elementary school teachers and students, this study could not have been accomplished. Finally, the authors wish to thank the reviewers for their many helpful comments, direction and suggestions.

This research was completed by the first author in partial fulfillment of the requirements for a master's degree in the Department of Speech Communication (Communication Disorders) at the University of Maine.

Bibliography

Abbs, P. (1987) 'Towards a coherent arts aesthetic', in P. Abbs (ed.), *Living powers: the Arts in Education* (pp. 9–66). Lewes: Falmer Press.

Ackerman, D. and Mount, H. (1991) *Literacy for All.* London: David Fulton Publishers.

Aherne, P. (1990) *Communication for All.* London: David Fulton Publishers.

Allen, A. and Coley, J. (1996) *Dance for All.* London: David Fulton Publishers.

Allen, M., Kertoy, M., Sherblom, J. and Pettit, J. (1994) 'Children's narrative productions: a comparison of personal event and fictional stories'. *Applied Psycholinguistics*, **15**, 149–176.

Applebee, A. (1978) *The Child's Concept of Story.* Chicago: Chicago University Press.

Arnold, M. (1960) *Emotion and Personality.* New York: Columbia University Press.

Aspin, D. (1981) 'Assessment and education in the arts', in M. Ross (ed.), *The Aesthetic Imperative: Relevance and Responsibility in Arts Education* (pp. 25–52). Oxford: Pergamon Press.

Baron-Cohen. S. (1993) 'From attention-goal psychology to belief-desire psychology: the development of a theory of mind, and its dysfunction', in S. Baron-Cohen, H. Tager-Flusberg and D. Cohen (eds), *Understanding other minds: perspectives from autism* (pp. 59–82). Oxford: Oxford Medical Publications.

Barrs, M., Dombey, H., Frater, G. and Johnson, J. (1993) 'The new National Curriculum for English', *Language Matters*, (**3**), 21–23.

Baumgart, D. (1992) 'Principle of partial participation and individualised adaptation in educational programmes for severely handicapped students', *Journal of the Association for Persons with Severe Handicaps*, 7(2), 17–27.

Berman, R. (1988) 'On the ability to relate events in narrative', *Discourse Processes*, **11**, 469–497.

Bishop, D. (1997) *Uncommon Understanding: Development and Disorders of Language and Comprehension in Children.* Hove: Psychology Press.

Bloom, L. (1993) *The Transition from Infancy to Language: Acquiring the Power of Expression.* Cambridge: Cambridge University Press.

Booth, T. and Booth, W. (1996) 'Sounds of silence: narrative research with inarticulate subjects', *Disability and Society*, **11**, 55–69.

Broadbent, S. (1995) *Key Stage 3 English Units: Materials for Learning and Assessment.* London: English & Media Centre.

Brown, E. (1996) *Religious Education for All.* London: David Fulton Publishers.

Bruner, J. (1986) *Actual Minds, Possible Worlds.* Harvard: Harvard University Press.

Campion, C. (1997) *An exploration of Cummins' theory of basic interpersonal skills and cognitive academic language proficiency, relating to bilingual children with special educational needs.* M.Sc., University of London Institute of Education.

Carpenter, B. (1997) Introduction, in *Literacy through symbols.* London: David Fulton Publishers.

Carpenter, B., Ashdown, R. and Bovair, K. (1996) *Enabling Access: Effective Teaching and Learning for Pupils with Learning Difficulties.* London: David Fulton Publishers.

Clark, E. (1973) 'Non-linguistic strategies and the acquisition of word meaning', *Cognition*, **2**, 161–182.

Coupe, J. and Goldbart, J. (1988) *Communication before Speech.* London: Croom Helm.

Cox, B. (1995) *Cox on Cox: the Battle for the English Curriculum.* London: Hodder and Stoughton.

Crystal, D. (1997) 'Language play and linguistic intervention', *Child Language Teaching and Therapy*, **13**, 328–345.

Dearing, R. (1994) *The National Curriculum and its Assessment.* London: SCAA.

Department for Education and Employment (1998) *The National Literacy Strategy: Framework for Teaching.* London: DfEE.

Detheridge, T. and Detheridge, M. (1997) *Literacy through symbols.* London: David Fulton Publishers.

Department of Education and Science (DES) (1975) *A language for life* (Bullock Report). London: HMSO.

Department of Education and Science (DES) (1989) *English for ages 5 to 16.*

Department of Education and Science (DES) (1995) *The English National Curriculum.* London: HMSO.

Department of Education and Science (DES) (Kingman Report) (1988) *Report of the Committee of Inquiry into the Teaching of English Language.* London: HMSO.

Dewart, H. and Summers, S. (1995) *The Pragmatics Profile of Everyday Communication Skills in Children.* Slough: NFER Nelson.

Dewart, H. and Summers, S. (1996) *Pragmatics Profile of Everyday Communication Skills in Adults*. Slough: NFER Nelson.

Dixon, J. (1994) 'Categories to frame an English curriculum', *English in Education*, 28, 3–8.

Dombey, H. (1993) 'Some thoughts on the proposals for Reading', *Language Matters*, 3, 15.

Dunbar, R. (1997) *Grooming Gossip: the Evolution of Language*. London: Faber and Faber.

Fabbretti, D., Pizzuto, E., Vicari, S. and Volterra, V. (1997) 'A story description task in children with Down's syndrome: lexical and morphosyntactic abilities', *Journal of Intellectual Disability Research*, 41(2), 165–179.

Fitzpatrick, J. (1988) 'Literature and special needs in the primary school', in T. Roberts (ed.), *Encouraging Expression: Arts in the Primary Curriculum* (pp. 105–130). London: Cassell.

Fox, C. (1993) *At the Very Edge of the Forest: the Influence of Literature on Storytelling by Children*. London: Cassell.

Franks, A. (1996) 'Drama, desire and schooling: drives to learning in expressive school subjects', in Vygotsky-Piaget (1996) *Second Conference for Socio-cultural Research*. University of Geneva.

Fyfe, C. (1996) *New Horizons*. Unpublished.

Geertz, C. (1983) *Local Knowledge: Further Essays in Interpretive Anthropology*. New York: Basic Books.

Goleman, D. (1996) *Emotional Intelligence*. London: Bloomsbury Press.

Golinkoff, R. and Hirsh-Pasek, K. (1995) 'Reinterpreting children's comprehension: toward a new framework', in P. Fletcher and B. MacWhinney (eds), *The Handbook of Child Language*. Oxford: Blackwell.

Goodman, E. (1981) 'Aesthetic developments in the visual mode', in M. Ross (ed.), *Assessment and Education in the Arts* (pp. 53–75). Oxford: Pergamon Press.

Gough, M. (1993) *In Touch with Dance*. Lancaster: Whitehorn Books.

Green, C. and Reid, D. (1996) 'Defining, validating and increasing indices of happiness among people with profound multiple disabilities', *Journal of Applied Behaviour Analysis*, 29, 67–78.

Greenhalgh, P. (1994) *Emotional Growth and Learning*. London: Routledge.

Grove, N. (1995) *An exploration of the linguistic skills of signers with learning difficulties*. Ph.D, University of London.

Grove, N. and Park, K. (1996) *Odyssey Now*. London: Jessica Kingsley.

Grove, N. and Park, K. (1997) 'Exploring poetry', *PMLD Link* (July).

Hardy, B. (1975) *Tellers and Listeners*. London: Athlone Press.

Heath, S. B. (1982) 'What no bedtime story means: narrative skills at home and at school', *Language in Society*, 11, 49–76.

Heathcote, D. (1984) 'Considerations when working with mentally handicapped people', in L. Johnson and C. O'Neill (eds), *Dorothy Heathcote: Collected Writings on Education and Drama* (pp. 148–156). London: Hutchinson Education.

Hemphill, I., Feldman, H., Camp, I., Griffin, T., Miranda, A. and Wolf, D. (1994) 'Developmental changes in narrative and non-narrative discourse in children with and without brain injury', *Journal of Communication Disorders*, 27, 107–133.

Hester, H. (1993) Editorial. *Language Matters* (3), 1.

Hicks, D. (1990) 'Narrative skills and genre knowledge: ways of telling in the primary school grades', *Applied Psycholinguistics*, 11, 83–104.

Hicks, D. and Wolf, D. (1988) 'Texts within texts: a developmental study of children's play narratives', in *Papers and Reports on Child Language Development*. Stanford: Stanford University Press.

Hobson, P. (1993) *Autism and the Development of Mind*. Hove: LEA.

Ireland, C. (1997) Foreword. In S. Parr, S. Byng and S. Gilpin (eds), *Talking about Aphasia: Living with Loss of Language after Stroke*. Buckingham: Open University Press.

Johnson, C. (1995) 'Expanding norms for narration', *Language, Speech and Hearing Services in Schools*, 26, 326–341.

Jordan, R. and Libby, S. (1997) 'Developing and using play in the curriculum', in S. Powell and R. Jordan (eds) *Autism and Learning: A Guide to Good Practice*, 28–45. London: David Fulton Publishers.

Karmiloff-Smith, A. (1985) 'Language and cognitive processes from a developmental perspective', *Language and Cognitive Processes*, 1, 61–85.

Kelleher, A. and Mulcahey, M. (1986) 'Patterns of disability in the mentally handicapped', in J.M. Berg (ed.) *Science and Service in Mental Retardation: Proceedings of the 7th Congress of the IASSMD*. London: Methuen.

Kerbel, D. and Grunwell, P. (1998a) 'A study of idiom comprehension in children with semantic-pragmatic difficulties. Part I: Task effects on the assessment of idiom comprehension in children', *International Journal of Language and Communication Disorders*, 33, 1–22.

Kerbel, D. and Grunwell, P. (1998b) 'A study of idiom comprehension in children with semantic-pragmatic difficulties. Part II: Between-groups results and discussion', *International Journal of Language and Communication Disorders*, 33, 23–44.

King-DeBaun, P. (1990) *Storytime: Stories, Symbols and Emergent Literacy Activities for Young, Special Needs Children*. Park City, UT.: Creative Communicating.

Knight, R. (1996) *Valuing English: Reflections on the National Curriculum*. London: David Fulton Publishers.

Knowles, W. and Masidlover, M. (1982) *The Derbyshire Language Scheme*. Derbyshire County Council.

Labov, W. (1972) *Language in the Inner City*. Philadelphia: University of Philadelphia Press.

Labov, W. and Weletsky, J. (1967) 'Narrative analysis: oral versions of personal experience', in J. Helm (ed.), *Essays in the Verbal and Visual Arts* (pp. 12–44). Seattle: University of Washington Press.

Lancioni, G., Reilly, M. and Emerson, E. (1996) 'A review of choice research with people with severe and profound developmental disabilities', *Research in Developmental Disabilities*, 17, 391–411.

Locke, A. (1985) *Living Language*. Windsor: NFER Nelson.

Loveland, K. and Tunali, B. (1993) 'Narrative language in autism and the theory of mind hypothesis: a wider perspective', in S. Baron-Cohen, H. Tager-Flusberg and D. Cohen (eds), *Understanding Other Minds: Perspectives from Autism* (pp. 244–266). Oxford: Oxford Medical Publications.

Lunzer, E. and Gardner, K. (1984). *Learning from the written word*. Edinburgh: Oliver and Boyd.

Macleish, A. (1961) *Poetry and Experience*. London: Bodley Head.

Mandler, J. and Johnson, N. (1977) 'Remembrance of things parsed: story structure and recall', *Cognitive Psychology*, 111–151.

Mandler, M. (1992) 'How to build a baby II: Conceptual primitives', *Psychological Review*, 99, 587–604.

McCabe, A. and Peterson, C. (eds). (1991) *Developing Narrative Structure*. Hillsdale: NJ: LEA.

Meringoff, L., Vibbert, M., Char, C., Fernie, D., Banker, G. and Gardner, H. (1983) 'How is children's learning from television distinctive? Exploring the medium methodologically', in J. Bryant and D. Anderson (eds), *Children's Understanding of Television: Research on Attention and Comprehension* (pp. 151–177). New York: Academic Press.

Merrick, B. and Brennan, J. (1993) 'Signals from magic stones', *Support for Learning*, 8, 112–115.

Moore, L. (1997) *Reference and representation in Down's syndrome*. Ph.D., University of Plymouth.

Musselwhite, C. (1990) 'Topic setting: generic and specific strategies', in *Fourth Biennial International ISAAC Conference on Augmentative and Alternative Communication*, Stockholm, Sweden.

Musselwhite, C. and King-DeBaun, P. (1997) *Emergent Literacy Success: Merging Technology and Whole Language for Students with Disabilities*. Park City, UT.: Creative Communicating.

National Curriculum Council (1991) *Aspects of English: English in the National Curriculum in Key Stages 1–4*. York: NCC.

National Curriculum Council (1992) *The National Curriculum and Pupils with Severe Learning Difficulties: NCC Inset Resources*. York: NCC.

National Curriculum Council (1993) *English in the National Curriculum: A Report to the Secretary of State for Education on the statutory consultation for attainment targets and programmes of study for English*. York: NCC.

Nelson, K. (1973) 'Structure and strategy in learning to talk', *Monographs of the Society of Research in Child Development*, 38 (serial number 149).

Nelson, K. (1986) 'Event knowledge and cognitive development', in K. Nelson (ed.), *Event knowledge: Structure and Function in Development* (pp. 87–118). Hillsdale, NJ: LEA.

Nind, M. and Hewitt, D. (1994). *Access to Communication: Developing the Basics of Communication with People with Severe Learning Difficulties*. London: David Fulton Publishers.

Oakhill, J. (1994) 'Individual differences in children's text comprehension', in M. Gernsbacher (ed.), *The Handbook of Psycholinguistics*. San Diego, CA.: Academic Press.

Park, K. (in press). 'Dickens for all: inclusive approaches to literature and communication with people with severe and profound learning disabilities', *British Journal of Special Education*.

Peach, L. and Burton, A. (1995) *English as a Creative Art: Literary Concepts linked to Creative Writing*. London: David Fulton Publishers.

Peter, M. (1994) *Drama for All*. London: David Fulton Publishers.

Peter, M. (1996) *Art for All*. London: David Fulton Publishers.

Peterson, C. and McCabe, A. (1983) *Developmental Psycholinguistics: Three Ways of Looking at a Child's Narrative*. New York: Plenum.

Protherough, R. (1983) *Developing Response to Fiction*. London: OUP.

Ray, R. (1996) 'Creative writing workshops for all', in J. Piotrowski (ed.), *Expressive Arts in the Primary School* (pp. 10–23). London: Cassell.

Reilly, J., Klima, E. and Bellugi, U. (1990) 'Once more with feeling: affect and language in atypical populations', *Development and Psychopathology*, 2, 367–391.

Rinaldi, W. (1992) *Social Use of Language Programme: enhancing the social communication of children and teenagers with special educational needs*. Slough: NFER Nelson.

Rosen, H. (1988) 'Responding to Kingman', in E. Ashworth and L. Masterman (eds), *Responding to Kingman*. Nottingham University, 21st June: Nottingham University School of Education.

Ross, M. (1978) *The Creative Arts*. London: Heinemann Educational.

Roth, P. and Spekman, N. (1984) 'Assessing the pragmatic abilities of children', *Journal of Speech and Hearing Disorders*, 49, 2–11 (Part 1); 12–17 (Part 2).

Rumsey, J., Rapoport, J. and Sceery, W. (1985) 'Autistic children as adults: psychiatric, social and behavioural outcomes', *Journal of the American Academy of Child and Adolescent Psychiatry*, 24, 465–473.

Schneider, P. and Dubé, R. (1997) 'Effect of pictorial versus oral story presentation on children's use of referring expressions in retell', *First Language*, 17, 283–302.

Sedgwick, F. (1992) 'Getting it true: notes on the teaching of poetry', in T. Booth, W. Swann, M. Masterton and P. Potts (eds), *Learning for All I: Curricula for Diversity in Education*. Oxford: OUP, Routledge.

Snow, C. (1983) 'Literacy and language: relationships during the preschool years', *Harvard Educational Review*, 53(2), 165–189.

Sperber, D. and Wilson, D. (1986) *Relevance: Communication and Cognition*. Oxford: Blackwell.

Spinillo, A. and Pinto, G. (1994) 'Children's narratives under different conditions: a comparative study', *British Journal of Developmental Psychology*, 12, 177–193.

Stein, N. and Glenn, C. (1979) 'An analysis of story comprehension in elementary school children', in R. Freedle (ed.), *New Directions in Discourse Processing*. Norwood, NJ.: Ablex.

Swanwick, K. (1997) 'Assessing musical quality in the National Curriculum', *British Journal of Musical Education*, 14, 205–216.

Tager-Flusberg, H. (1993) 'What language reveals about the understanding of minds in children with autism', in S. Baron-Cohen, H. Tager-Flusberg and D. Cohen (eds), *Understanding other Minds: Perspectives from Autism* (pp. 138–157). Oxford: Oxford Medical Publications.

Vance, M. and Wells, B. (1994) 'The wrong end of the stick: language-impaired children's understanding of non-literal language', *Child Language Teaching and Therapy*, 10, 23–46.

Wade, B. and Oates, M. (1993) 'Shakespeare for all?' *Special Children*, March, 8–11.

Webb, E. (1992) *Literature in Education: Encounter and Experience*. London: Falmer Press.

Weir, R. (1962) *Narratives from the Crib*. The Hague: Mouton.

Westby, C., Dongen, R. V. and Maggart, Z. (1989) 'Assessing narrative competence', *Seminars in Speech and Language*, 10(1), 63–75.

White, H. (1980) 'The value of narrativity in the representation of reality', in *On Narrative* (pp. 1–49). Chicago: University of Chicago Press.

Wiig, E. and Secord, W. (1996) *Test of Word Knowledge*. London: Psychological Corporation.

Wills, P. and Peter, M. (1996) *Music for All*. London: David Fulton Publishers.

THE LIBRARY
SWINDON COLLEGE
REGENT CIRCUS

Index